Changing your life when you don't know how or where to start

J.L. James

WHO IS THIS BOOK FOR?

For anyone suffering in silence every day. You have the strength to rise up. Whilst it may not seem like it now, being a victim is a choice.

You have the courage to fight every day. The strength to be the confident, empowered person you always wanted to be.

If you have made the choice to stop being a victim, the following pages are for you. If you aren't ready yet, keep this handy for when you are.

There will come a day when you will be ready to start the journey to rise up.

Remember, always look forward – never back.

Disclaimer

The information in this book is based on the author's own experiences and knowledge. It is not a substitute for professional advice in any area covered. The author cannot be held responsible for any loss – direct or indirect, claim or damage arising out of use of the information contained herein.

DEDICATION

'He's just a bully. Those two little boys are watching everything you two do. You are showing them this is normal behaviour. They will grow up to be exactly like him. One day, we may not get here in time. You have to find the strength to confront him. Believe me, like all bullies, he will crumble'. **Police Sargent who changed, and saved, my life in the early 90s.**

I dedicate this book to him. He didn't just save my life and that of my children that day, but all the people I've helped empower to change their lives on The Real Apprentice, Growing Talent employment programmes, bespoke positive mind and wellbeing workshops I've devised and delivered and the hundreds of hours spent as a Shout Volunteer on the crisis text line Give Us A Shout helping vulnerable people find their path to move from a hot moment to a cool calm.

WHAT IS THIS ABOUT – IS IT FOR ME?

In essence, it's a road map on how I faked confidence to get to where I wanted and needed to be.

There was no manual on how to manage life, relationships, bullying, legal issues, children, jobs, council housing etc when I needed it.

This covers some of the things I've discovered along the way. I hope it helps you make the choices that are right for you.

It isn't life events that impact us, but our decisions on how we react to those events.

There is always a solution. There is always choice. You are strong enough.

CONTENTS

BACKGROUND

I don't doubt some or all of you will unfortunately be able to relate to some of the areas I cover in this book. Know this. You don't have to settle for less than you want. It will take effort and you will never feel like doing the hard work to secure the change you want. Knowing that is half the battle.

I was at primary school when the bullying started. I had the whole package. Fat, greasy hair, spots – that I picked urgh! – clean but old clothes and clearly an overload of shyness. There was a song at the time called 'Hey Fatty Bum Bum' by Carl Malcom released in 1975. It rode high in the charts and seemed like it was on the lips of every other kid in school every time I walked by!

I knew my family loved me but saying it was just 'puppy fat' didn't help. I still had my sweets every day! It was a vicious cycle – the more I was bullied, the more I ate. The more I ate, the fatter I got and the more I was bullied. Thank goodness there was no social media then. At least the bullying stopped outside of school.

I remember a school journey to Sayer's Croft. We shared small chalets. When I say chalets – more like fancy sheds. Absolutely not remotely acceptable by today's standards. But at the time it was deemed to build confidence and character. From memory I was about 9. Mum sent me a big box of sweets which I know was money she could not afford. Of course, I shared these with all 'my friends' who flocked to the chalet I was in on seeing a big package arrive and left as soon as they had their sweets. I felt so empty. The rest of the time was one of the most miserable and lonely periods of my life.

I was too fat to run fast so wasn't picked for the sports games. With more spots than a dalmatian dog I wasn't pretty so not accepted by the popular girls. To me, I wasn't worthy of 'friends.

My self-esteem – although I didn't know it was called that at the time – was zero. When I got home, my loneliness continued. I started writing suicide notes to myself. At the time I had no idea that's what they were I just felt so hopeless and worthless and didn't want to feel like that anymore I just wanted the empty feelings to stop. Today I look back and can still feel the pain of my younger self.

I've spent over ten years as an Instructor in mental health. Undertaken ASIST (Applied Suicide Intervention Training) for adults and ASK (Assessing Suicide in Kids).

In addition, I'm a Shout Volunteer with a crisis text line and support people through their suicidal thoughts. All of this training together with over twenty years in the resilience and wellbeing field help me support others but the most effective tool, I feel, is being able to relate to those feelings I had back then and my understanding now that suicide is a permanent solution to what is a temporary problem.

Something someone in pain can't always see.

Today we are thankfully more aware of mental health issues. There is great signposting to charities like Papyrus, Shout etc, GPs are more aware and everyone is starting to be more aware of how important mental resilience is. Then it was a case of don't tell anyone. Why? I don't know but I never told anyone until now.

I now recognise that total lack of self-esteem made me ripe for the bad decisions I made like getting engaged at 17 to someone I should have given a very wide birth to!

We were engaged for over two years before arranging the wedding in just three weeks. Why the rush at the end of this engagement? Even then, with little self-esteem, I knew deep down if I didn't marry him then, there was a chance I would listen to the others and find the strength to call the wedding off and everyone who continually told me it wouldn't work would be proved right.

It's funny, walking up the aisle at 19, knowing you want to call it off yet still walking towards the alter. Even the vicar came out and asked if I was sure – if that wasn't a sure sign not to go ahead, I don't know what was.

With everyone sitting in the church – the overriding compulsion was I couldn't let them down. As I entered the church in the crinoline style lace dress my mum had worked on day and night to get finished in just three weeks – I absolutely couldn't let her down.

My nan had made the octagonal shaped three tier wedding cake with intricate icing. Like mum, nan had worked day and night to produce this beautiful cake. I couldn't let her down either – could I?

My dad's best friend was by my side as we entered the church. He had five boys and was unlikely to get another opportunity to walk a bride down the aisle – I couldn't let him down, could I?

'Hell yes'! I'd scream at that 19 year old now!

The stupid thing was each of them would have been so happy if I'd called the wedding off. They were all highly aware of the situation I was walking into.

Life events can strip away our self-esteem to a point of removing the clarity to see clearly and the strength to do what we need to. We cling on to people who disempower us because we feel it's what we deserve.

He was my first boyfriend and I'd met him just three weeks after my beloved dad had died after a two year horrific battle with cancer. My brother and sister had both left home long before. My mum, being just 43 at the time my dad had died, was naturally grieving. We'd all been on the most horrific journey. Today of course, there would be automatic grief counselling. Talking about feelings is so much more cathartic than trying to deal with them alone. We would have had very different lives had we had that counselling. However, history cannot be re-written. We must learn from it and move on. No matter how long it takes to do so.

FAKING IT UNTIL YOU BECOME IT!

I have used this consistently throughout my life but only discovered Dr Amy Cuddy sharing the science behind this in 2019!

Let's go back a little. At 19, I was a newly-wed working at an advertising agency in Soho Square. A beautiful building facing the green square. Each road from the square led to an interesting part of London.

One contained a Hari Krishna temple with a vegetarian café. Many of us got lunches for there long before Quinoa became popular. In the opposite corner were Walt Disney offices. Down another exit to the square, was a night club. The whole area was cosmopolitan and exciting for a sheltered 19 year old! I loved it.

One event illustrated the need to 'seize the day' as there is no guarantee what each day will bring. I remember some of the team returned in tears from a lunchtime trip to Oxford Street – not that far away on the tube. They described a loud rumble and utter chaos. Bearing in mind there was no social media then so news didn't spread as quickly. It transpired a bomb disposal expert was blown-up whilst trying to diffuse an IRA bomb. I did a Google search for the purpose of writing this. His name was Kenneth Howorth. The date was 26 October 1981. Train and tube stations were chaotic. Police were everywhere. You could almost touch the fear in the air that day.

Today it's hard to imagine a time before the peace process when expecting bombs to go off in London was just part of working there. Something you just dealt with. I remember speaking with an Irish friend some years later who said prior to the peace agreement they would not speak in public for fear of others knowing they were Irish and seeing them visibly move away.

I really loved working at the Agency and I especially loved working in London. The sights, sounds and even dirt just make it strangely comfortable – still to this day. It's a unique Capital City.

The Agency has long gone but was quite innovative at the time. The CEO's PA had one of the first word processors. In the early 1980s these were the size of a table and revolutionised office work.

Now we can compose and send documents on our smartphones and tablets! I was one of the director's audio secretary with an electric typewriter, carbon paper and tippex – dried up bottles – this was before the innovative tippex stripes come along.

I was fully aware as a newly-wed my obligations were to bring in as much money as possible. While the job at the Agency was fun it wasn't a great salary.

I saw a job advertised for £1,000 more annual salary and decided to apply. A short time later, the interview letter came through. Oh lord. I hadn't read the original job advert properly. It didn't require an Audio Secretary but an Audio Word Processing Secretary to manage a team of 5 tax account managers.

It was one week before the interview. Luckily the CEO's PA at the advertising agency agreed to give me a few quick lessons. Remember – cut and paste were unheard of for a typist! The day of the interview came.

I arrived at the London Bridge office of this global accountancy firm in my best interview dress (aka only interview dress!) After what felt like an informal chat with the Administration Team Manager, I was led into the test room.

Picture the scene - before me were two huge word processing machines – the size of dining tables! - with their even bigger printer in the middle. They looked pretty similar to the PA's one so I started to relax a little.

The test I had to undertake involved typing a passage then bring up another document cutting and pasting that into the text and saving it. One of the things I hadn't been shown was how to save a document! Talk about anxiety! My mouth was dry, heart racing, palms sweaty as hell.

'How do you think that went?' asked the interviewer. 'Ok, I think. I'm so sorry about the save function. I've been trained on a different machine – but I'm a quick learner'.

We chatted a little more before she turned to me and said 'you kept really cool under pressure there, which is what this job needs looking after five managers. Just for your information, there is only one word processing machine in existence'

Ouch! I'd been rumbled but 'faking it until I made it' worked. I was taken on and worked for the company for two years before leaving to have my first child. Again, I was so happy here. The team became like family to me.

We had such fun during those two years. There was about six of us in the 'word processing pool' – think typing pool in the retro films on tv! We felt more like family. I learned the art of communication here. Getting to know my five managers, meant I could learn more by being flexible which in turn gave me more flexible lunch hours!!!

We all had two senior managers and then 2-3 juniors. If we wanted to go shopping during our lunch hour to Lewisham or the Old Kent Road – a mum of one of the other girls in the 'pool' had a clothes shop there and gave us good discounts – we would arrange with the managers to give us as much work as they could leading up to the 'shopping day'.

As we got ahead with our work, they didn't mind letting us have a 2hour plus lunch hour! They even covered for us with the 'pool manager'!

Getting to know all my managers and treating them with respect and interest gave me the same treatment back. It also delivered an effective, professional and mutually beneficial working relationship. A key learning element we don't always see in others is that no matter how senior someone is or how rich they are, they are human too and have the same worries as anyone else – maybe on a different scale. Communication is not only essential in the workplace, but in life as well.

If I was going for that interview now of course I'd research and be prepared. But faced with a similar situation, I'd always 'fake it' – you might just pull it off. Working for that company would have a profound effect on my later life.

It's amazing looking back, how very quickly and deftly the confidence I'd gained was systematically erased. Mental abuse is very different to physical abuse in that the wounds never heal totally. 30+ years later, I can still relate to the fear and worthlessness I felt then. I didn't see it coming and the slow evolvement meant I soon felt the relationship and how I was treated was normal.

Brainwashing is a cancer for humans. It zaps our control and smothers our self-esteem making us a shell of our former selves. Of course, others will try to help but no one in that position listens at the time. Like magnets, the pull of loyalty and 'this is what I deserve' is too strong. They have to find the strength within themselves to break away.

The marriage lasted ten years. My children were 6 and 4 at the time of the break-up. Dumped for an older model I'm not sure if that is more insulting than a younger model would have been!

Although I wasn't at the time, I am so grateful to the other woman later for so determinedly setting out to get him. Although it was a five year struggle after we split up with police and court battles before finally getting free of him, I am thriving now and so are my children – which would not have been the case had the marriage survived.

So I found myself looking for a job after building up a business and home for 10 years. I'd walked away with the boys and a court order for £15 for each child until they completed full time education or reached 18. This order was only honoured for six months! I'd asked Social Security (there was no JobCentre Plus then) for some help until the course I was on completed in four weeks. I had a job lined up after this. The chap on the end of the phone told me 'no, you're young - go and get married again'. That wouldn't happen now but his attitude fired me up.

It was down to me to ensure my children grew into kind human beings with integrity and for me to carve out a career. Getting a 'real' job was easier said than done when you are judged by your labels – such as single parent, unemployed and so on.

For me a 'real' job is permanent with good pay and conditions, in a safe environment with training and development opportunities to grow that job into a career. A job where I was a respected member of the team treated equally and respectfully.

Something every adult is entitled to in my view. This seemed impossible to get back then when judged by labels. Employers – and people in general – learn of someone's labels and immediately make assumptions. For single parent many assume - ' 'kids by different men', 'irresponsible to get pregnant', 'lives on a sink estate', 'unreliable'. Even though today we have a lot of legislation, some people will still make assumptions about you without even knowing you. This I see every day in my work with vulnerable people.

As a 'real' job was unattainable for me in the initial period after the split and benefits weren't an option, I embarked on a series of low paid, cash in hand jobs, often two or three jobs at the same time, in not always the safest environments. What mattered was feeding my children. Pride had to take a back seat. Still the seed of determination was growing with each knockback.

On top of this, the Court ordered the sale of the marital home with him bearing any shortfall on the mortgage. This was during a recession in the early 90s. I never wanted to buy the house in the first place due to it being dead opposite the shop. However, he was insistent and I didn't have the self-belief to fight him.

We brought the house for £87K. The court ordered the sale for 'the best price' a local estate agent could get – which was £49,000! I later learned from an ex-neighbour that the £30K shortfall was paid in three cash payments! So, my children and I were officially homeless and on the homeless list for re-housing. People hear the term 'homeless' and immediately think of those living on the street but the term includes sofa surfers, people in temporary accommodation and families like mine where their home had been ordered sold and they had no home of their own. The anxiety and fear of where we would live, how we would cope grew in waves.

The Council's Homeless Persons Unit explained they would make one offer and only one offer. My heart sank when I saw that offer. A two bedroom flat on the top floor of a rundown block built just after the war. The previous tenant was a drug addict who was removed via eviction after starting a fire.

Whilst the flat was bad, I had already been warned there would be no further offers if I didn't accept the tenancy. I couldn't risk putting the children into a worse situation. We moved in without a stick of furniture. The Council's Homeless Persons Unit gave us vouchers to buy basic quality paint and wallpaper.

Thing to remember when you are rock bottom, the only way to go is up. The flat was awful. I felt such a failure taking the boys from their comfortable home close to their school to this empty shell but it felt safe, was ours and he didn't have keys!

What I learned was children don't need material things. They just need to feel loved and safe. Whilst we had nothing, looking back, we actually had everything. We were the three musketeers. I know from working with homeless people now who have to go into a bidding system, just how lucky we were back then to get that offer.

THE CRAWL BACK TO EMPLOYMENT

Whatever 'real' job I applied for, the response was always the same. I'd worked with my ex building up a business which was solely in his name. I couldn't get a reference and the years spent building the business up seemed to count for nothing. As far as employers were concerned I had no relevant experience for the previous 10 years and no reference on my performance. It's the age old issue – you haven't got the experience but how can you if no one gives you a chance?

Of course, on reflection, as we know any employer will train new employees if they have the enthusiasm they seek, I now know it was my labels and employers' assumptions of those labels putting them off. As any of you reading this who have or have had 'labels' previously, will agree we are the most committed, reliable people because we really, really, really want the opportunity and won't waste the chance if it's actually given to us.

I carried on with the numerous cash in hand jobs I'd secured, sub-contracting delivering catalogues, cleaning etc being paid a fraction of the going rate and never knowing how long the job would last. With no benefits, I couldn't afford to be choosy. I knew I was being taken advantage of but I was feeding my children and keeping a roof over their heads. Again, this situation wouldn't arise now. On reflection I am glad the Department of Health and Social Security's rep (predecessor to JobCenter Plus) said that to me all those years ago about re-marrying. It taught me to keep fighting and pushing forward – even if I was faking it confidence wise!

I carried on with all these bits and pieces of jobs whilst the boys were young. As they grew, I knew I had to get a 'proper' career started otherwise I would always be stuck in the spiral of unsafe, poorly paid jobs with no future.

I'd heard about a new accountant practice starting up locally above a hairdressers. Shaking like a leaf, I'd put on my best charity shop clothes, devised my cv and marched in through the door. Faking it big time! Here's how the conversation went.

Remember, there was no accounting software then. On seeing a sea of carrier bags containing lose receipts for each customer, feigning confidence I said (remember the word processing job from earlier) "I can help you get all of this in order. I've been trained by a global accountancy firm. Let me work for you for a week. If at the end of that week, I've been a benefit to you, you pay me and give me a permanent part-time job to fit in with my children's schooling. If I haven't helped, I'll walk away and you don't pay me. What have you got to lose?"

The young accountant was also a new father who had recently set-up as a sole trader. He gave me a shot. I worked for him for over four years. Sometimes you have to 'fake' your confidence until you actually become confident. It really does happen – believe me. I share some tools on how to 'fake it' in the following pages. Do give them a try.

Of course, money was tight but without the pressure of walking on egg shells constantly everything was so much brighter. I would go to upmarket areas to buy the boys clothes from charity shops although they always had new underwear and shoes/trainers! Even if you can't afford to wear designer clothes, there is no reason not to look smart, clean and tidy. I got over my aversion of charity shops by thinking how most of us buy new clothes. Go in the shop, try your size on and buy it. We don't think of washing it before wearing it even though other people have likely tried it on before us.

We had to be clever with food shopping too but more about that later.

My experience up to this point became the foundation a few years later for devising The Real Apprentice and later the Growing Talent employment programmes. Both programmes enabled unemployed people to showcase their hidden talent whilst growing in confidence on their journey from unemployment benefits into work without being judged by their 'labels'.

The Real Apprentice started in 2004 and ran until 2013 winning multiple awards, year on year – including the best of Europe -beating 23 other countries – in the employment initiative category. I'm proud to still see some of the Real Apprentices about in London still working for the employers they joined over ten years ago , although now in different roles.

Growing Talent was devised at the end of 2013 following an approach from an employer involved in the Real Apprentice. Hopefully it will re-start after the pandemic restrictions are removed. Check out more about this at www.growing-talent.co.uk.

Combined, close to 1,000 people from all backgrounds have grown their self-esteem, skills and secured permanent employment which literally changed their lives for the better through these two programmes. Something I'm immensely proud of.

Until you make the decision you want to be the strong, independent person you know you are on the inside and actively change your mindset, nothing will change. I'm still a strong believer in faking it until you become it and use the techniques in my training of others – including management level of staff - as well as unemployed talent.

The following pages cover what I've learned and include some of the key areas I now teach others who are in a similar place I was. A place where 'labels' are seen more than the people behind those labels.

Ever been judged for being a single parent or homeless or jobless or having some other label? You know that look in people's eyes when they learn your label. The assumptions and judgements you see they make without even really knowing you.

I hope this helps you deal with those looks, how they make you feel and unlock the power within you to move forward with your head high empowered by that spark of wanting to be the person you know you really are – strong, courageous and kind.

Mantra

Mantra or mission statement gives us a solid foundation for the journey to our goals. A simple sentence that means something to you – doesn't matter if someone else said it first. It hasn't got to be unique and clever. Just something that ignites that fire in you. Something that when you say it over and over you feel the empowerment within you growing. The more you repeat your mantra, the smaller that negative voice in your head will become and the bigger the positive, invincible side will grow.

The official definition of a mantra – which is originally thought to come from Hinduism or Buddhism – is a word or sound to aid concentration in meditation. For me, a mantra re-focuses my mind when negative thoughts intrude my thinking.

I used and still use the Serenity Prayer as my mantra. Different sources talk about where this started. Some think the Army. I don't know where it really started, and does it really matter? I first saw it on the back of a St Christopher necklace my parents gave me as a child.

It goes something like this….

'O God grant me the *serenity* to accept what cannot be changed, *courage* to change what should be changed and the *wisdom* to distinguish one from the other.' I was blind to that message for many years.

Practising my mantra has stopped me wasting energy on things I cannot change.

Easier said than done sometimes but when we really think and analyse what it is we are worrying about, it makes it easier to weed out the small stuff.

Why not think about a mantra/mission statement for yourself? Write it down on a piece of card and carry it around with you. Alternatively, take a photo on your mobile – it's always accessible to look at and reinforce that positivity. You could make it your screen saver. Why not print posters with your mantra on and display them in every room of your home to constantly amplify the positive message.

How do you work out your goal?

You may know you don't want to be where you are. Whether that's professionally or personally. Some of us will have personal, educational, professional goals. It's not always easy to know where we want to be and how to get there.

Working out our goals is the key issue. How can we plan our journey if it's goalless? Without goals we can't plan the vital elements of researching and preparation for the journey.

There are some tools we can use which we'll look at later including our own roadmap, finding our why etc.

Goals are on-going and changeable. As we reach one goal – more will spring up. The empowerment of reaching your fist goal and pushing through to the next is indescribable.

Accept the need for goals in all areas of your life, throughout your life.

EDUCATION

Having worked with diverse cultures over the years, I'm aware how amazed they are by the attitude of some of those young enough to have free education in the UK who don't seem to value it. They feel some take the notion of free education for all is a given right that some don't make the most of. Whereas in their ancestral countries their parents have to pay for their education which makes the sacrifice an additional 'pressure' to take education seriously. In some countries outside the UK some families can't afford to educate all of their children and choose to educate just their sons – even if their daughters have more aptitude to learn.

I totally see how they feel. I admit I didn't make the most of my free education. Many families in the UK don't take education for themselves or their children seriously. If you live in poverty or in a low income family or in an area of high deprivation with negativity all around you – think coastal/ex-mining towns – the key to escape the circle of deprivation and helplessness is education, yet there is little encouragement to take it up. Why? I'm not sure what the answer is. It's been this way for generations. The one good thing is the opportunity to learn privately as we grow older and get more respect for education.

There is no age limit to learning. At both my sons' graduations there were people collecting their degrees and doctorates in their retirement. Continuous learning keeps our minds active and has been proven to stave of dementia. Of course, we don't have to do higher education to keep our minds active. Learning any new skill does the same thing and opens up a whole new network of contacts and friendships.

From going to see the Biggin Hill Air Show at about eight I wanted to be a pilot – not in the Forces but an airline pilot. I knew I needed to gain good qualifications including in science before going to University for further study.

Teachers can have a long lasting impact on students – not always a good impact. Large classroom sizes, overwork, admin, family lives – who knows what turns a passionate teacher into someone just killing time no longer interested in moulding young minds. Even when education is free across the UK, the quality can vary hugely. Prior to a new science teacher joining my secondary school, I was enthused and hungry to learn more. Unfortunately, this new teacher sucked my enthusiasm out of me and ended my dreams of being a pilot at that point.

It seemed life was also conspiring against my dreams of being a pilot. Around this time my dad was diagnosed with cancer. I was 15. Unlike today, treatments were harsh and often ineffective stripping the person's spirit at the time. There was no financial help or support for my parents at that time either – unlike today.

As the last child at home, I dropped any ideas of university and got a job in a bank a month before my 16th birthday. After my dad's death when I was 17, I decided to re visit my education with private lessons to secure English A level and German.

I found a father and daughter tutor tag team - who were like chalk and cheese in all areas. Both were so interesting in polar opposite directions and both taught me so much beside English and German. The daughter had the top floor in the family home. Refined with a love of art and ballet she was well travelled and so interesting to talk to on multiple subjects apart from English – her specialist area. She opened my mind to question more.

Her dad was just as powerful. He always had a cigarette in the corner of his mouth which never seemed to move when he spoke – this was before the legislation not to smoke indoors. A broad Yorkshireman who always wore a vest – no shirt. He spoke five languages and prior to retirement worked internationally for Governments and corporate businesses. Something you would not have thought based on his appearance. We are all guilty of judging someone without getting to know them. We can learn not to do this. Having been judged on my labels in the past, I know how painful and inaccurate this can be. I strive to resist the urge to make assumptions. It's as simple as just stopping, asking yourself what evidence you have to think that way and then have a conversation with that person to reveal the truth.

Again, life got in the way of these studies with the arrival of my first boyfriend (later to be husband mentioned previously). I only secured O level in English down to my lack of enthused study. I dropped my German studies altogether which really disappointed my tutor who had termed me a 'Meister' of German after just a year of study.

At the time I worked for a company called ITT in their International Data Engineering department. With offices in Stuttgart, I practised my language with colleagues based there over the phone – who were all encouraging. I could translate written German into English with ease too. I was influenced to give my studies up by the drip feed of negativity from said boyfriend.

What's the point in sharing this? A few things really.

- If you don't make the most of education when you are young – that's not the end. You can learn and train no matter how old you are.

- People are rarely what we assume they will be. By listening to people without judgement our minds can be opened to new views, horizons and goals.

- It doesn't matter if we were influenced to believe we are worthless. We can change, grow and do anything we want to.

In general, I've always felt it strange that we ask a young person to know what they want to do with the rest of their lives at 16. What subjects will you study? What career are you going into? Are you going to University, getting a job or starting an apprenticeship? No one ever knows exactly what they want to do with their lives at 16. Wouldn't it be better to have a 2-3- year break at 16 and return to free education when you have a better idea of what you want to focus on?

The education system in the UK leaves a lot to be desired to me. It seems completely skewed towards academia which to me seems unbalanced and definitely not inclusive. Many children are not academic but they have a natural flair to the arts or an inquisitiveness toward understanding how things work. Why do we insist on judging young people by how many exams they pass? We don't even teach them a subject only to pass an exam.

For adults, the opportunities to re-train and secure qualifications later in life shows where education in the UK excels for me. A variety of options from The Open University, online courses, private tuition, part-time/evening study through Birbeck University or other institutions. There are multiple access courses to reach degree level if required once adults realise the industry/career they do want to work in.

I never did get to university but I've ended up in a career in inclusive employment, mental health and well-being which seems to be my niche. It's not been a career I sought or planned, instead it sort of evolved as I was offered opportunities along the way. However, it's given me so much – confidence, self-esteem, financial independence, the opportunity and platform to change hearts and minds. My advice to anyone is be open to every opportunity. You have no idea where it might lead – I didn't.

If you are reading this and thinking 'I wish I'd worked harder.' Stop. There is always a way to achieve what you want to do. Plan for it but be adaptable with the hiccups and hurdles that will present themselves along the way. Do it and ignore the naysayers around you. This is your only life, not a test run.

In March 2020 lockdown in the UK arrived. Coronavirus had started a few months earlier in China and spread globally. Lockdown brought enforced reflection. Growing Talent, the key part of my work at the time was put on hold. Understandably, no employer was recruiting. Other clients who had training confirmed – cancelled.

Discussion with my client saw a virtual Growing Talent conceived and a virtual journey book produced! A new animated film was made and the format shortened to five weeks. As the lockdown progressed further, I started to look at enhancing Growing Talent's wellbeing offering as well as adding some accredited services to my business offering. Change and adapt – key words for us all.

Let me take a moment here to explain Growing Talent so you can understand the desire I had to make everyone on it feel they have been invested in and have something meaningful by completing in addition to a permanent job.

Growing Talent is unique in a number of ways. There are no cvs nor formal interview. It is an opportunity for someone with little confidence and 'labels' to grow as they learn with the support of a dedicated mentor and the comfort of retaining their Universal Credit.

The USP (unique selling point) of Growing Talent is, if selected to take part by an employer, a permanent job is ring fenced which the individual trains in during their time on Growing Talent. Whilst on Growing Talent, participants kept their full benefits and had all their travel paid. If the fit wasn't right, they simply went back to their obligations with JobCentre Plus without having to make a new claim. This 'try before you buy' concept resulted in confident recruitment because both the individual and the employer could test each other out before hiring. The attraction for JobCentre Plus is their clients leave benefits in a more sustainable way. A robust orientation and holistic element delivers life skills including self - empowerment

A typical Growing Talent programme goes like this:

Initial information sessions and sifting by JobCentre Plus managers who then issue the application form where applicable.

1-2-1 compatibility meeting to ensure applicants are right for the programme and the programme is right for them. On average for a programme with ten applicants – the cost to my budget was over £3,500 per head. This stage is crucial. There is no automatic right to secure a place just because someone is unemployed and referred by JobCentre Plus.

Speed dating session - first stage selection. All applicants who have completed initial compatibility screening meet all employers in small groups to share a snapshot of themselves and learn key aspects of the employers and roles on offer.

1-2-1 with employer. Any shortlisted by the employer meet them where the role is based for a more in-depth meeting. Meeting the team and seeing the environment enables the decision to be made on whether to accept the offer or not based on location, environment and 'feel' of the role, travel times etc.

Combined Orientation and Holistic week – those offered a place who accept undertake this combined week learning new skills and growing in confidence before going onsite and training in the vacant role with the employer and their team. I delivered the MHFA Adult course as part of this section. This gave all a certificate of attendance. A certificate is really important for some of the participants on Growing Talent who for one reason or another didn't complete their formal education. The MHFA courses – Awareness – half a day, Champion – one day and Adult – two days is a global reactive product to raise understanding of what to do is someone exhibits potential signs of mental ill health.

Whilst I was confident all areas of the orientation and holistic sections are robust, the reactive and non-accredited status of the MHFA course troubled me.

I wanted a meaningful course to match MHFAEngland's three levels – Awareness, Champion and First Aider courses – but they had to carry accreditation. I found Nuco Training which matched what I was looking for. Accredited by Ofqual all manuals are electronic so easy to deliver virtually and globally. FAA Level 1 is equivalent to MHFA's Awareness course, FAA Level 2 equivalent to the Champion course and finally FAA Level 3 – matching MHFA's Adult two day course.

There was a hurdle first. To be accepted as an Instructor to undertake training for Nuco's three courses, I had to have Level 3 qualification in Education and Training! A year long course, which I thankfully completed in three months! I then embarked on the Instructor training with Nuco and passed! Returning to the world of formal academia where lesson plans, risk assessments etc had to be thought about was new, challenging and ultimately refreshing.

At the same time, I wanted a ***proactive*** programme designed for the workplace which focussed on wellbeing therefore reducing the risk of mental ill-health issues arising. Investigation revealed i-act – an excellent programme with two key courses would be the answer. The first course is aimed at managers with team responsibilities. The second aimed at individuals with no team leadership duties. Both courses have over 50 selfcare tools and are accredited by Royal College of Psychiatrists. As an Instructor, I would be able to deliver both - Understanding and Promoting Mental Health and Wellbeing as well as Managing and Promoting Positive Mental Health and Wellbeing. Both courses also have a robust manual for onward learning and access to i-act's website for updates.

Apart from the valuable knowledge I was gaining doing these Instructor training courses, I made some great connections globally including Afghanistan, Bahrain and Hong Kong. I can't explain the empowerment I feel setting and achieving these small challenges for myself. It's something I aim to continue long after the restrictions of this pandemic are lifted.

Going forward, the proactive and accredited courses of i-act will be delivered as part of Growing Talent. The self-care tools will be invaluable to people on the programme and enable them to help others in the future.

I really recommend you set yourself some goals with timelines. We can all do more than we think we can. Don't let your negative mind creep into your thoughts!

Changing how we work has been so exciting – yet slightly scary at the same time. Depending on how we look at it as individuals.

I think of the actor Will Smith's quote "Success is on the other side of fear" – whenever doubt enters my mind. Yes, that's right. There are times when I start to doubt myself even now – it doesn't last long.

We can all control our minds rather than our minds control us. We just have to want to.

RELATIONSHIPS – professional and personal

Like anything relationships take preparation, research and practice to get right. For me the key ingredient for all relationships is self-esteem. If we don't have that personal self-belief, we are in danger of building toxic relationships and living our lives without joy in a feeling of permanent quicksand. This, I believe, is reflected in personal and professional relationships.

Our building bricks for relationships are built in the home by families as we grow-up. If we have a nurturing, caring family around us we will inevitably grow into a strong, empathetic and resilient adults. By family, I mean those looking after this. It may not be a mother and a father. It can be two mums, two dads, a single parent, grandparents or friends.

From what I've seen and the people I have worked with over the years, it really doesn't matter who makes up your family but it does matter that they love, nurture and care for you grounding you in kind principles to live by and a solid belief in yourself.

Have you noticed how babies get what they need? They cry for everything they need but only have a few needs – a cuddle (we all need to be loved), hungry, thirsty, wet, too hot (babies rarely cry when they are too cold so we need to be mindful). They aren't worried about world peace, politics, the latest pram, designer clothes or anything else. They focus on what they need.

If the family communicate by shouting at each other, the baby grows up thinking that's the norm and grows into a screaming child and potentially a narcissist adult. We've all seen the fruits of this with parents unable to reason with their children – reap what you sow springs to mind! Of course, if children recognise their family's behaviour isn't the norm, they can learn better communication techniques.

Let's reflect for a moment here. Have you ever seen a frazzled adult with a child that appears to be disruptive? Would you think that's a spoilt child that the parent can't control? Many would think that was the case. Or would you think, that person looks exhausted, I wonder if their child is neurodiverse? This could just as easily be the case.

For me, this illustrates the human condition to judge people without finding out the facts first. How many of us have ignored situations like this and how many have asked if any help is needed? I'm reminded of a story a few years back. A person was travelling on the train. Opposite them they saw a woman travelling with two children, one of whom was loudly shouting and 'acting up'. Everyone was staring at a woman as if asking her why she wasn't doing anything to control her child. He saw how exhausted she looked.

Imagine how alone that woman felt. The person went over and spoke to the child making the noise. They ended up doing a drawing challenge which focussed the child and calmed them down leaving the woman and remaining child to have their drinks in peace. The woman was so grateful to the person for engaging their neurodiverse child leaving them to focus on their other child. Turns out the person who intervened had a younger neurodiverse brother and knew from their own experience what was going on.

Shouldn't we check ourselves before jumping to conclusions? Do we like others making assumptions about us? Just how great would this world be if we showed a little kindness to each other.

We saw above how babies learn from other adults on how to communicate. Adults can just as easily learn from young children.

Go into any nursery and you will see children from all races, religions, abilities and social backgrounds playing together. As we were all that age once, where does our assumptions, discrimination and segregation thoughts come from as we grow?

Check out some key skills in the Communication section. Silence and avoidance can be a key indicators someone is struggling with something they feel uncomfortable talking about. Remember, we are a cosmopolitan country with a diverse population from all corners of the world. Some will embrace the UK's traditions and drop their traditional tribal customs. Others won't. This causes a whole range of problems for children born and/or brought up in the UK to families who still practice age old traditions.

Experiences like FGM (female genital mutilation) – there are over 300,000 girls and women in the UK who have experienced this. Although this has been illegal in the UK for years, only one parent has successfully been prosecuted. Arranged marriages, honour violence, honour killings, non-acceptance of being LGBTQ+ and so on. All of these issues happen in the UK now.

We often fall silent when we think this is going on for fear of being deemed racist. How is it acceptable for someone to struggle alone between the culture of their home in the UK and the traditional practices of their family? No one should have to remain silent because of fear. No one on the outside should hesitate raising the alarm because they feel they will be judged.

If you fall into any of these categories, don't live in continued fear. Check out the resources at the back of this book and reach out for help. You deserve to live your life the way you want to in peace and without fear. Being stuck between two cultures must be horrendous but help is available.

Be aware of those around you. If you notice any change in their behaviour, plan an approach to find out if they are struggling and need support. They might just be having a bad day but asking, whatever the cause, shows you care and are approachable. If you are particularly interested in how to do this, check out my website for information on courses you can consider – www.janejamesconsultancy.com.

ACCEPTANCE - something we have to do – no matter how much we struggle to do so

I look at the elderly many are frail and alone. How many have families who are preoccupied with their own families to show their parent(s) they care? Every parent has to accept they are no longer needed once their child becomes a self-sufficient adult.

Covid has thrown a spotlight on the loneliness caused. It's not always easy doing things for yourself when you've always put others first. But then as time progresses on, I'm reminded, even in the happiest, most loving relationships, the odds are at some point one of a couple will be left alone. There's an element of acceptance in the ending of any relationship whether it's through break-up, death, one partner having to go into a care home or when someone in an abusive relationship – physical, financial, emotional – makes the decision they have to leave.

Accepting this change and finding an identity as just **you** again is very tough. I think the first step is acceptance. The glib saying, we come into this life alone and we leave it the same way, rings true and logical, however, some of us will live many years alone and lonely if we don't plan what we will do when we are left alone, we can no longer work, illness takes over, children are grown and no longer need us or something else happens to change our purpose in life. If we don't have a purpose in life, life just becomes the passage of time.

It's important to always evolve as an individual. To grow and learn. To always have a purpose. Our purpose will not stay the same. It will change.

Asking for appropriate help when we need it at every stage of our life is so crucial. It's a strength not a weakness. If you need help of any kind – check out the resources at the end of this book. Don't suffer in silence.

The quicker we accept things the quicker we can move on. Change is going to happen. Are we going to be proactive or reactive?

Key points in relationship communication – professional or personal

*Considerations where you are **doing** the talking:*

- Are your feelings fact or perception?
- What is your goal in having this conversation?
- What is the best method to use for this conversation – face-to-face, written, phone call?
- Where and when is this conversation going to take place?
- What words are you going to use?
- What are the possible consequences to what you are going to say?
- Do you have any possible resolutions to what they might say?
- Are you prepared for any emotions you might encounter as a result?
- What's your emotional status? – are you calm enough to have this conversation?

*Considerations when you are **receiving** the communication:*

- Have you summarised and reflected back to the person what they've said to ensure you've understood them correctly?
- If you feel negatively about what they've said, tell them – give them the opportunity to explain more clearly.
- If what they have said really upsets you, resist the urge to continue the conversation. Explain you are shocked and need to re-convene later. A pause will enable you to reflect on what's been said along with your feelings and clarity to respond accurately rather than knee jerking through emotions.
- Remember, someone's intention may be lost in the words/tone/body language they use.

Any communication without thought and preparation will generally fail to meet its goal.

GETTING A JOB WHEN YOUR 'LABEL' IS SEEN FIRST

So far, we've looked at the initial stages of starting again and starting my journey to employment. Now we look at some key issues I encountered which you may be able to relate to.

How do you get a job when you don't have recent and/or relevant experience, lack self-confidence, have a 'label(s)' which enables some to pre-judge you and not see the skills and qualities hidden by these labels coupled with no recent employer to give you a reference?

Example of how our qualities may be hidden by our labels:

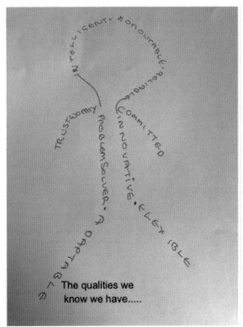

The qualities we know we have.....

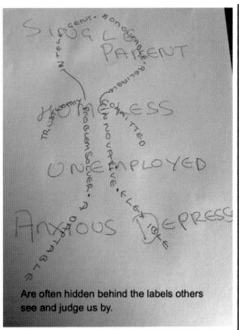

Are often hidden behind the labels others see and judge us by.

The first step for me to move forward was to recognise change started with me – no one else. I had to stop seeing myself as a victim, weak with numerous labels and start seeing myself as a survivor, a warrior who had achieved many things alone and believe I had a lot of qualities valuable to employers.

I realised I couldn't convince employers to have confidence in me and give me an opportunity until I believed in myself.

All the time I allowed the negativity I'd been fed for years to remain the loudest voice the longer my labels would be seen.

Sound familiar?

It's not an easy task, takes courage and a fake it attitude – which when you have 'labels' is especially tough - **but it is achievable**. Everyone's journey to a job and hopefully a career they enjoy is different. We are all in the storm of life but in different boats. Let's not beat ourselves up nor constantly compare ourselves to others. Even with a total lack of self-esteem, we can move forward by using a few tools.

The following is what worked for me and what I use in the employment programmes I've run over the years to enable people in difficult circumstances with 'labels' to get the job they want, take control of their lives and move on.

We've looked previously at mantras to keep us focussed. Later we'll look at some great tools to kickstart your journey ahead. These include power breathing and visualisation to manage anxiety and the 5,4,3,2,1 method to counter procrastination (overthinking) and some self-care tools.

First let's consider some steps to getting a job. Preparation is always key to everything. The following steps will be different for each of us depending on our personal circumstances.

Step one - Understand why you need/want a job.

- Do you purely need to earn money to pay bills so any job will do?
- Want to identify the first step onto the path of your chosen career?
- Social ethos is more important than financial considerations?
- Want your own identity to be seen in your own right?
- To make friends and keep your brain active?

Your reason may be one of the above a combination or something completely different. Knowing your reason helps you identify the right role and sector.

Step two - Work out what industry you want to work in.

If you don't know, work out what you don't like and then consider what's left. Volunteering in different industries, networking (remember this is just another word for talking) with those that are already in that industry and learning the different roles in that sector will give you accurate information on where your path lies. Remember, this won't be set in stone. Paths don't always go in a straight line. Other opportunities may open up along the way that you hadn't considered. That's ok. Change is to be embraced nor feared.

Be prepared for trying a number of industries and roles before finding the one that is for you.   A free resource you may like to check out is www.careershifters.org founded by Richard Alderson. Dis-illusioned with corporate life, Richard wanted a change but didn't know what. After trying several shadowing opportunities with his existing contacts and volunteering in different industries he found his niche in the social entrepreneurial area. He founded Careershifters to help those navigating where they want to be career wise.

Step three – pathway considerations

Do you need to secure qualifications/training – what is the best institution for this? What qualifications are most recognised and fit your lifestyle and the career/industry you have in mind. Is there a series of qualifications you need or just one?

Finance – how are you going to pay for the course and live whilst re-training? There are a number of potential options.

You can stay in your job and save enough to pay for your course and keep yourself for the duration.

- Is sponsorship available?
- Could you reduce your hours at work and study part-time?
- Can you keep your day job and study evening/weekends through flexible universities example Birbeck in London or online?
- If you want to start your own business, can you do this alongside your day job until you feel confident enough to leave your day job and focus full-time on your new business? Is there any funding available for starting your own business?

Flexible Schedule – looking at your end goal only can be so huge it becomes overwhelming leading to you dropping your new path. Instead plan your schedule and be flexible. You might have to adapt it as you go along. Life, family, friends won't stop for your plan. Having a series of smaller goals and a time line to achieve each will give you the visual focus to stay on track. Be sure to build in self-praise for each goal you achieve. Building a new career and changing our lives takes strength and courage. It's a marathon – not a sprint. You've got this!

The following pages contain exercises and tools to help you work through these steps.

FINDING YOUR WHY

Take some time to work out what your purpose is. What brings you joy? What do you love getting up in the mornings to do, miss lunchtimes for – get totally immersed in it without much effort? You may know this already. If you don't consider:

1. What do you do well with the minimum amount of effort?

2. Think about someone in your past who made a positive impact on you. Recount your memory of them to someone close to you. Ask them to notice when you 'light up' as you talk about them. This will be at the point you mention the quality you admired most in them. This quality could be your 'why'.

3. Compose an Ikigai diagram. Lots of videos on YouTube. In essence, take an A4 sheet of paper. Mark a horizontal line in the middle and a vertical line so you end up with four squares. Put one of the following statements in each box and then fill the box. You will likely see a specific item, repeated in each. This could be your 'Why'

    - What are your passions?
    - What are you good at?
    - What can you can earn money from?
    - What does your community need?

Ikigai example – writing is exposed as the specific item in each quadrant. Could that be the purpose to focus on?

What are my passions?	**What am I good at?**
People, gardening, nature, Learning, writing – books, how to guides etc	Coaching others Writing courses, handouts, manuals Empowering others
What does my community Need	**What can I make money at?**
Unity, security – financial & homes, knowledge on how to change their life – written guides	Writing and publishing how to guides Selling garden produce

4. Ask your friends what quality stands out about you from their other friends?
5. Think about this quality and compose a statement on what your purpose is:

"To_____ so that _____"

First blank is your contribution. Second blank is the impact.

Example: 'I propel people forward so they can make their mark on the world' David Mead – Co-Author of Start With Why. Simon Sinek is the other Co-Author. Check out their books and videos on YouTube – great resources.

ROADMAP STEPS

Start where you are: note down work, home, leisure, what are you happy with/what do you want to change?

Where you want to be: What is your goal? How will you know you've reached it? What small targets along the way?

Now, fill in the gaps with all the steps you need to achieve with timelines to get up to where you want to be. Remember, this might take years. Nothing worthwhile happens overnight. Apart from a lottery win maybe – and just how likely is that? Note down your successes as this will spur you on. Now we all know life is not a straight line. You need to be prepared for curve balls. So in your plan, have some 'what ifs' in mind – 'what if this happens? – I'll do that.'

Example of my Roadmap when Coronavirus hit the UK in March 2020.

Where am I now: Self-employed working in London delivering classroom based mental health, wellbeing, self-empowerment and employment courses.

Step 1:   Rewrite core programmes to deliver virtually within four months – **Done**

Devise series of wellbeing and empowerment workshops for virtual delivery – **completed by July 2020** with on-going commission requests

Step 2:   Look at accredited courses. Discover I have to have a Level 3 in Education & Training (1 year course) to deliver accredited Mental Health in First Aid.

Step 3:   Undertook L3 – completed and passed within three months - **Done**

Step 4:   Undertake i-act Instructor training – **completed and passed October 2020** Undertake and complete FAA levels 1, 2 and 3 Instructor training in First Aid – **completed and passed October 2020**.

Step 4:   Start to learn Spanish once Coronavirus restrictions are lifted in 2021

Step 5:   Get legal terms and GDPR drawn up by Solicitor for virtual training – **completed October 2020**.

Step 6:   Spend 2021 and 2022 delivering virtual courses as well as classroom based work

Step 7:   Spend two weeks each year in different areas of Lanzarote/Spain to see where I want to live in seven years' time. First area booked for May 2021 depending on the pandemic status. Moved to Christmas 2021 – thanks pandemic!

Step 8: Once fluent in Spanish – estimated 2023 – start offering virtual training in Spanish

Step 9: Join Spanish group to understand business opportunities, legal/commercial issues etc. Joined newsletter service. Will join formal group with membership from 2024.

Step 10: Continually upskill and save, save, save!

Where I want to be: In seven years, living in the hills of Spain delivering virtual courses worldwide from a base in virtually permanent sunshine.

Now I don't doubt some of the above will alter, and that's fine. I'm prepared for that. Having a few steps already completed inspires me to push on. Try it. See if a roadmap works for you. You can use a flow chart, picture diagrams – whatever works for you. A roadmap should be unique and meaningful to you. It will propel you forward, give you structure and a continual purpose.

Misconceptions on why we don't get a job?

'I never get a job as I don't have experience' – I hear this a lot from all ages and backgrounds whether it's someone's first job or a career change. Personally, I think, unless it's a particularly specialist job, this is a smokescreen excuse. Ask yourself this - if you had your own business making apple pies and the two candidates below present themselves which one would you choose?

Candidate A – Long-time very experienced baker, who can make a great apple pie, quiet, unenthused personality who gives one word answers.

Or

Candidate B – passionate about cooking in general. Loves fresh ingredients. Eager and passionate sharing their cooking triumphs – and disasters! Good sense of humour.

I suspect, like me, you'd choose Candidate B. Ask any employer what they want when recruiting new talent. All will say the same. They want a positive, enthused attitude who wants to learn their business. They will train so previous experience is at the bottom of their wish list. In fact, many prefer those with no experience in their industry so they aren't having to 'de-train' bad methods taught previously.

Work on showcasing your positivity mentioned earlier is essential to you securing your next opportunity. You really do have to fake it until you make it sometimes! Concentrate on showing the interviewer how committed and enthused you are.

STRATEGIES TO CONSIDER TO SECURE A JOB

It's key to know the purpose of each stage to ensure you focus and prepare for it strategically.

Some people make the mistake that one cv will do and its only role is to secure you a job. This could not be more wrong. The cv's only role is to get you an interview. That's it. You still have to showcase your personality, skills, commitment and potential to secure the role.

It's a key tool to showcase your enthusiasm, transferable skills and the value you will add to the business. There are some effective subtle techniques we can use in the cv to give us a better edge to selection. We'll explore these in the cv format section.

To really standout, you need to prepare and research. Spending time to make sure the foundations of a house are strong enough to take the weight ensure the house will stand for years. Having a technique to ensure each cv you send is bespoke will stand a better chance of you securing an interview at which you get the opportunity to secure the role.

Skills Map

Don't make the mistake of heading straight into composing your cv without first composing a Skills Map. **Its job is to capture every skill and attribute you have in one place.**

This was a method I used when thinking how can I 'sell' myself into a 'proper' job at the start of my journey.

I took a sheet of paper and divided it into two columns. In the first I listed all the jobs I had before getting married, any volunteering I'd done and studies. I then listed my role as a single parent, interaction with the legal profession (aka getting a divorce) and running a house with a limited budget. In the second column I listed all skills and attributes associated with the first column. If you prefer, you can split column 2 and have a dedicated skills column and a third column for attributes. This is a matter of personal choice so long as you investigate and capture all.

After a couple of hours, I had robust lists for each column and was empowered by what I had done and enthused at the diverse skills I had.

None of this was obvious to me prior to doing the Skills Map. There's something about seeing written evidence that's empowering. Compiling my Skills Map enabled me to see the job title I used which captured all the diverse skills I'd accumulated – Director of Household Services – impressive, don't you think? It captures the role of someone running a household who is bringing up children more aptly!

Consider if you had to employ someone to run your house and/or look after your children. So many skills are involved and their wage would be way above the minimum wage. Yet you do all of the roles involved without thought or payment. You are the expert of your household. The skills and experience you reveal doing your Skills Map will be invaluable to employers and empower you.

I advise everyone on my employment programmes to do their own Skills Map. Storing this living document on the computer enables you to continuously update the document as more skills and attributes are gained in new roles . Once compiled, selecting the matching skills and attributes for each role you apply for in the future is easy and accurate.

Let's take a generic example of a Skills Map

Computer games	Hand to eye co-ordination
	Proactive
	Problem solving
Volunteering charity shop	Display of products
	Stock control and rotation
	Customer service
	Customer resolution
	Cash/card handling
Online diploma	Time management
	Self-motivation
	Research, investigation and analysis
	Report compilation
Unemployed/raising family	Household management
	Finance projections, budget control
	Event planning, scheduling
	Risk management
	First aid
Shop Assistant	Customer communication
	Issue resolution
	Team interaction
	Cash/card payment processing
	Display of goods
	Stock rotation, ordering, processing
	Product knowledge and marketing

As you can see, you soon get a number of skills and attributes you won't have thought you had that are highly attractive to employers. Of course, you won't know how any of these translate into the employer's business – but the fact you already do the same in a different environment proves your attitude to learn.

Before you start internally belittling your achievements – something every human with little or no self-esteem does – remember the employer is happy to train in their business. You weren't born knowing how to run a house nor bring up children. Why talk yourself out of being 'trainable' when the evidence is there to prove the opposite to you?

Find a quiet time to compile your own Skills Map. Of course, this is easiest on a laptop/desktop. However, not everyone has their own computer equipment. Don't worry, you can get the same affect by using pen and paper. You just need to keep the finished document safe. You might want to take a photo on your mobile of your completed Skills Map as a back-up.

After compiling your Skills Map you should have the evidence to help you devise your personal brand and elevator pitch. Both help your cv flow and enable you to enhance your professional profiles on social media.

Personal brand

Is literally what someone would think about you on reading your social media profiles. Are you passionate about the Environment? Communication? Food? Be clear on what you stand for. Check out the personal brand films on YouTube to give you an idea. Make sure all of your social media accounts give the same personal brand feeling.

Elevator pitch

Is pretty much what it sounds like. A summary of you that you can convey to someone in 30 seconds – the average elevator journey. Short and snappy. It is not a summary of your cv! It's a snapshot of you. A taste of your talent and what you offer so the person you are talking to wants to know more. Again, YouTube is your friend here.

These first three steps will give a solid foundation to now compile your cv.

CV thoughts

Ask any recruiter or HR professional, no matter what style they individually prefer, they will all agree you have the first half page of a cv maximum to gain their interest and increase the chance of being called for interview. It's no good putting a key alignment with the advertised job/company at the end of your cv as it likely won't be read! Opportunity missed.

Make sure you use the language the employer uses in documentation sent to you or uses on their website. This creates a subliminal link to you. In addition, sifting software and speed readers look for key words linked to the job vacancy – not just the job title. Make use of these indicators to raise your chances of selection to the next stage.

Example: a leading facilities management company had the following strapline a number of years ago : *'people + passion'*. This was used on their website, in all marketing and their social media profiles. If I was applying for a role with them at the time, I might have started my profile/personal statement with:

'I am **passionate** about working with **people** to deliver a seamless service to our clients…'

Another thing to bear in mind in compiling your cv is the Equalities Act 2010. Don't risk being discriminated against by putting irrelevant information on your cv. For example, your age or anything that can reveal your age – such as years you were at secondary school is irrelevant unless you have recently left full-time education.

With the half page limit in mind, I know that sounds tough but that is how long you have to get the reader's interest, its' important to make this section count. Consider the following techniques in compiling your cv having already completed your Skills Map, personal brand and elevator pitch:

Bearing in mind what we know on time taken to read/scan cvs - you might want to consider the following format which will get all key information within the first half page sweet spot:

Let's look at the skeleton outline of the cv format before looking at each step in a little more detail:

- Name
- Location
- Contact details
- Social Media account
- Personal profile/statement
- Column 1 – skills   Column 2 – Attributes
- Employment history
- Education/training
- Interests
- References

Name – your usual name.

Location – can be just your town or postcode - you don't have to disclose your full address at this stage if you prefer. Leaving this blank will often remove you as the employer/recruiter will have no idea where you are based into relation of their role. Example – they could be in London whilst you are in Newcastle. People are not mind readers. Make it easy by giving an area/postcode of where you live.

Equally, if you do currently live outside an area you want to work in but plan to move there on securing a job – make this clear. Maybe something like 'currently located in Newcastle but planning to move to South East London shortly'. You may receive a call to explore more about this so think ahead. If you are called for interview, how much notice would you need to attend? If you were offered the role, do you have someone to stay with initially in the new location or do you need time to find somewhere before being able to start the now job. These are all questions you will need to have thought about and be able to provide confident answers to.

Contact details – email and mobile – make sure both are professional. As much as your friends might feel hotstuff@hotmail.com is cute – it's unlikely employers will!

Equally, employers and recruiters generally have huge responses to their vacancy adverts and little time to chase applicants they want to meet. Therefore, make it easy for them and less likely you will miss an opportunity you want by not being contactable. Have an answer facility on your mobile with a short message from you – not a long music intro. Remember your genre of music may not be shared by the employer/recruiter. Don't risk it! Your answer message is not a time to be unique and individual. It's a time to be efficient and professional. Maybe something like:

'Thank you for calling (your name). I value your call but I'm not available right now. Please leave your name and number - I will call you on my return later today.' Make sure you do return their call on the same day. It shows your interest and professionalism.

Social media account – employers/recruiters will search for you online to see what your 'presence' is like. They want to see if what you've put in your cv matches your presence. Therefore, it's important to check your privacy settings. If you haven't already, start a professional blog/LinkedIn account to put the link on your cv which they can check. Make sure your LinkedIn account reflects your professional interests so it continues the theme of your cv and flows well. Ask yourself is your personal brand and elevator pitch reflected here?

Profile/personal statement – 3-4 sentences to show the value you add to the role they are looking to fill. Be dynamic and different. Don't waste time on generic terms like, reliable, committed, organised. You are unique. Your profile/statement should be too. The reader is looking for a match to their role. This area is a key one to show them you are 'the one'.

Example – if I was an entertainment team member on a cruise ship who wanted to apply for a role in a corporate welcome host role - I might use something like the following as my personal statement:

'An innovative outlook, strong communication skills, unique problem solving abilities, inclusive liaison at all levels are part of my DNA honed via five years delivering entertainment on global cruise ships. From your website I see your ethos matches my passion to deliver an exclusive customer experience. I believe I match your role role. Let's discuss.'

The example showcases key skills from past experience that will match pretty much any role but especially that of a Corporate Welcome Host likely to have interaction with diverse clients at all levels. Including a mention of the company's website shows an interest in the company. Matching the company ethos to my passion creates the subliminal match enhanced by using any language/strapline the company uses.

Add in the theme of your personal brand illustrated in your social media presence, this statement becomes even more potent.

Skills & Attributes – bullet list the most relevant of these for the role/company you are applying to. Column one should contain the skills you have. This might include any skills like MS Office, accounts payable software – the actual skills you have from the roles you've done previously. Adjacent to this is Column two is for attributes - the 'soft' skills you have. These might include highly organised, innovative, problem solving etc. Remember the company's mission statement and/or strapline used in the vacancy advert and on their website. Create the subliminal link mentioned earlier and use it throughout.

By the time the reader reaches this point they should be at the half page stage and have enough information on you to decide whether they read anymore and/or call you for interview. These columns are hugely important to get right.

Employment history – most relevant first, no more than 10 years, short story for each entry – what your role was, what you did, value you added to the business why you left – 3-5 lines for each job.

Education & training – most recent/relevant first. If you have a degree, there is no need to put 'A' levels.

Hobbies – always something you do solitary and something you do as part of a team. This shows the prospective employer you can work alone and as part of a team. It's the continuous thread of compatibility you need to show.

References – will be given on request.

This format ensures you capture all relevant information in the first half page. It's worth reminding you to use language the company uses on their website/documentation they have sent to you. This creates a subliminal connection. Bear in mind some companies use sifting software so make sure you are using key search words mentioned in the job advertisement within your cv to give you a great chance of getting through the selection process.

If you are applying to a specific industry, why not consider applying a different way? Instead of just using a cv to respond to an advertised role, why not consider something more bespoke to build a connection even where there isn't an advertised role you know about? Employers have created roles when they've met people they want in their business. Think about how you stand out?

Finance – Consider areas you particularly like or financial stories you've seen that resonate with you. To be unique and different, maybe considering writing a business proposal, steps to secure a deal, a paper on why takeovers are good/bad, how AI could be adapted for financial issues in lower income areas or a solution to a particular financial issue. Absolutely anything to show you really have passion for the industry.

Marketing – why not do a 2 minute personal brand video on you replacing the cv? Or do a magazine style cover page? Both capture all aspects of the cv in a more visual way enabling your creativity to shine through. Maybe take a particular issue in marketing, design a solution and make a short video on that?

Hair & Beauty – a portfolio on styles or different aspects of make-up – theatrical, camaflouge etc. Consider writing 'how to booklets', anything on specific issues in the industry you want to address. Set-up a YouTube channel and send the link to specialists you are interested in.

There are so many options when we stop thinking solely about traditional job application methods.

Covering letter/email – sole purpose is to get your cv read

The covering letter/email is the introduction of you to the employer. Key words to keep in mind when composing this are *short*, *snappy* and *unique*. It is not a summary of your cv.

There is no harm in being confident and challenging. Maybe something like:

'I've seen your role for………………………………. I know I have the skills and personality to be a valuable asset to your business. Let's meet for coffee and discuss'

Anything that challenges the employer to read your cv and ultimately meet you is a positive. Sometimes you have to be assertive to stand out – even if it is not your comfort zone. Remember 'fake it until you make it!'

Application forms

Please remember there are different protocols to cvs.

1.   All questions must be answered in full including your date of birth

2.   There can be no gaps in your employment history. Even if you've been long term unemployed or had various periods of unemployment, you need to list these. If you are currently unemployed, your work coach can give you the details of the central team who will give you a complete report on your signing history based on your National Insurance number. This can take a number of weeks to be produced so request it ahead of starting your career search.

3.   You have to be completely honest on an application form. For example, you cannot put 'education equivalent to GCSE' you must put your actual exams you attained.

Application forms are often online and very detailed. **Take your time**! It's a good idea to read through the whole form entirely and if possible save it, check spelling and content before submitting. As with cvs and covering letters always use language the company does. This aids the sifting processes and creates that subliminal link.

THE INTERVIEW – virtual and face-to-face

Coronavirus saw the rise of virtual interviews which may remain long after the virus has dissipated because of the cost and time savings virtual interviews bring. Some employers may use virtual meetings as part of their sifting process with face-to-face interviews remaining for second stage sifting.

Of course, many international companies have always used virtual interviews in their early selection stages for international staff applying for UK based jobs. Technology has introduced a new way of working for many. There are a few different considerations for each form of interview. Let's take a look at each. Remember knowledge is power!

Virtual interviews - Advance preparations and technical considerations

1.   Where in your home do you get the best wifi signal?

2.   What will your background look like? Can you have a virtual background? Does it look professional? Maybe upload your own photo which fits the role/company?

3.   What is the light like on your face in the location where you will have this interview? Remember the time of your interview and weather on the day could affect the light available especially if this is close to a window. Do you need to have additional light falling onto your screen from desk lights?

4.   Check out different positions to check you will be comfortable and raise your computer screen so you are not looking down which creates double chins!

5.   Having pre-read all the employer's documentation, compile a crib sheet to place next to your screen of key points you want to make as prompt if nerves kick in.

6.   What are you going to wear? Should be the same as if you were going for a face-to-face interview. If you are unsure of the dress code – call ahead and ask.

7.   Remember your body language.   Be aware of your habits – rubbing your face, fiddling hair, yawning, looking out of the window. Practice filming yourself on a platform like Zoom where you can set-up a free account. You will instantly see

any issues. By practising ahead of the interview you will be more comfortable with the software on the day.

8. Remember most people, including employers, are not mind readers. Employers will be grateful for advanced knowledge of anything you need which will enable you to get the most out of this virtual experience and you will feel more comfortable not having to try to mask any need you have.

Virtual interview – preparation on the day

1. Make sure all details of the role, employer and what you want to say are fresh in your mind with a quick read through.

2. Utilise the calming tools in your selfcare toolkit spoken about in this book. You will naturally feel a degree of anxiety and procrastination. Taking some time to power breath, power stand, visualiation – whatever your particular calming tools are - will empower you to give the best possible presentation of you possible.

3. Taking some time to focus your mind on the event, how the conversation may go, your preparation for various scenarios will get your mind in the zone.

4. Make sure anyone else in your home knows not to interrupt you.

5. Keep your mobile on silent away from your screen to avoid interference with signal.

6. Test your speakers before the interview ensuring the volume is at the right level.

7. Remember to mute yourself on joining the meeting and have your camera off until you are settled and ready to start a couple of minutes prior to the interview.

8. Have a glass of water close by – prevents dry mouths and gives you a few moments to think of an answer.

9. Make sure you observe all the points in your advanced preparation – seating position, lighting etc.

10. Make sure you are warm even if it means having a blanket over your knees!

Content of the virtual interview

This will largely follow the framework of the face-to-face content detailed further down. All interviews follow:

Beginning – introductions, settling you in, getting to know a little about you
Middle – the detail of the role, exploring how you match it and the USP you bring
End – round up. It's essential here to get a time line of when a decision will be made.

Face-to-face interviews

Ahead of the interview

- You cannot plan too much. Work out your route and a back-up in case there are transport strikes, cancellations, road works or anything else that can impact your timely attendance for your interview. Be mindful of timings. It's better to arrive too early and go for a walk locally rather than risk an option that gets you there just in time – if there are no delays.

- Compose a schedule for the day of the interview to enable everything to go as smoothly as possible.

- Re-read all documentation you have from the company and check-out their news tab on their website to compose your interesting and unique questions to the employer.

These questions might include:

- What attracted you to work for this company and why have you stayed?

- Can you tell me about the qualities of someone who successfully held this position before?

- What do you consider are the most important elements of the job on offer?

- Is there anything about the company you would change if you could?

- In the news tab on the company website it mentions European expansion. This sounds really exciting. Can you share some more about this – may what countries you are targeting first?

  These are more unique questions than what is the pay, benefits and training which are usually covered in the job description or advertisement sent to you. Asking these generic questions won't make you memorable and will make the interviewer feel you haven't bothered to read their documentation properly.

- Plan what you are going to wear and don't deviate on the day! Make sure what you choose looks good both sitting and standing. Check outfits in the mirror sitting and standing to help select the right one. As with virtual interviews, if you are unsure of the dress code, don't hesitate to call ahead and ask.

On the day of the interview

- Remember smell comes into face-to-face interviews so do not overdo perfume or aftershave. Whilst you may love it, the employer may not!

- Smokers – be mindful non-smokers can smell smoke on you very easily. Consider investing in some nicotine patches but don't try to mask smoke odour with an overload of perfume/aftershave.

- Don't eat on-route to your interview. There is nothing more off-putting than speaking to someone who has pieces of food stuck in their teeth. If you have a medical condition that requires you to eat very close to your interview time, take a toothbrush and toothpaste with you to brush your teeth on arrival.

- Take some time to get in the zone before entering the building by reminding yourself of the information you have on the company and role as well as how you fit.

- Get your mind calm and focussed by practising some of your selfcare tools – maybe power breathing, visualisation etc.

- Follow your schedule.

- Remember you don't know who you will pass on your journey so act as though you are in 'interview' the minute you leave your front door.

Let me illustrate that last point. Some years back I worked for an IT high-end recruitment consultancy. The Owner arrived back to the office a minute or two after their next interviewee arrived, very early, for their interview. I noticed a difference to the normal expression on the Owner's face. I sat in on the interview as a trainee.

The role we were recruiting for had a six figure salary with an annual bonus, healthcare and impressive car allowance. The Consultancy stood to earn well over five figures in recruitment consultancy fees if placement was made. The interview had gone very well, I thought. So, I was surprised when the Owner gave his feedback to the interviewee.

'Next time you are on-route to an interview, don't get aggressive and swear on your phone in the street and then spit on the pavement. I was behind you and know you are not the professional we have a reputation of putting forward to our clients.'

I'm not sure who was more surprised, me or the interviewee but I hope this shows you what can happen on route to an interview!

On entering the interview room

Thank the interviewer for meeting you. Tell them you are excited by the opportunity on offer and keen to learn more.

If offered a drink accept some water. If you are not offered a drink ask if it would be possible to have a glass of water or take your own small water bottle. Sipping water does a few positive things:

1. Keeps you hydrated – stress/pressure naturally releases Cortisol which gives the dry mouth we feel when under pressure
2. Gives your mind a couple of seconds to think of what you want to say
3. Will ease any unexpected tickly throats

Whilst you may prefer a hot drink, there is a risk of burning your mouth, spilling some on your clothes or not having enough time to drink it. Each will cause a degree of anxiety you don't need.

Remember the information covered in Communication and Body Language within this book. It's essential in showcasing the best version of you along with the preparation you did ahead of this face-to-face interview.

Make sure you listen to and answer the questions asked. If you are unsure what the interviewer means, ask them to clarify.

Some standard questions may include:

Tell me about yourself – include a snap shot of you professionally and personally, if you love working in a team, problem solving etc.

What is your key strength and weakness? Don't say 'my weakness is taking on too much work, not knowing when to say no or anything similar. This is so lame and the interviewer has heard it all before. Be more honest and give a solution. Example: 'I'm not very confident using Excel but have signed up to do an online course of an evening.'

Where do you see yourself in five years? 'Lying on a beach' or 'doing your job' are not great answers. The employer is looking for evidence you will stay. Remember it's costly for an employer to train you in their vacancy. There is a bigger cost to their reputation if they employ people who are going to leave shortly after.

If this is the job you truly want, consider something like 'for the first three years I see myself learning every aspect of the role on offer, how I can add value to it and the team and understand the wider business. For the following two years I would like to build on the experience and connections I have to work in other areas of the business adding greater value to the overall business at the same time developing my skills and experience with the company's guidance and training'.

Other competency questions may include any of the following:

- Describe a time you worked as part of a team to get something done
- Can you share an example of when you had to solve a problem?

- Give an example of how you make a decision
- Can you describe a time you had to meet a tough deadline and how you did it?
- Can you give an example of a time you had to use your initiative?
- What have you done that you are particularly proud of?

The final point – what are you proud of - can be conquering a family sponge cake recipe – it doesn't have to be anything major.

For all of the above remember the STAR format to give a well-structured and flowing answer – Situation, Task, Action, Result.

Once the interviewer has explained the role in-depth, asked the competency questions, they will ask if you have any questions. If they don't, say "I have a few questions I'd like to ask'. This is the time to ask your unique questions covered earlier.

Remember, before leaving the interview, thank the employer for their time, let them know you enjoyed meeting them and learning more about the role and company and ask when you can expect to hear. This gives you a timeline to follow-up.

Post interview – either virtual or face-to-face, make a note in your diary of when the employer told you they expected to make a decision. If you have not heard from them by this date, take the initiative and contact them.

Clothes – there is no second chance to make a 1st impression

It's worth spending a bit of time thinking about what clothes to wear for an interview – virtual or face-to-face. Preparing to give the best possible 1st impression of you, also makes you feel more confident and in control.

The whole image you present can work for you or against you. Think and prepare your appearance schedule in advance. It's no good trying a new brand of skincare, make-up or hair products on the day of the interview only to discover you are allergic. Resisting the urge to scratch, or trying to obscure red patches is a major distraction for all parties!

If you like a face pack or steaming your pores – do this a couple of days before with products you know. Whilst you won't have to deal with allergic reactions, having less to do on the day of your interview is more calming.

Depending on the time of your interview, you might have to do some tasks the day before so planning is key.

If you've been out of the employed environment for a long time, chances are you may not have 'appropriate' clothes. Whilst we saw in the skillsmap section there is a lot of cross over from running your home and raising children to qualities employers seek to their workplace – clothes is not always one of the crossovers! Whilst tracksuit bottoms etc are more comfortable, they may not match the employer's environment.

Do not rush out and borrow money/use credit cards to buy appropriate clothes. Many charities and JobCentre Plus can refer you to Smart Works or Suited and Booted. Both give you free unique guidance and interview clothes. Let's take a closer look at each:

Suited and Booted - www.suitedbootedcentre.org.uk based in the City of London

Founded in 2012 by Dr Maria Lenn to give vulnerable, unemployed and low income men help by giving the good quality used clothes donated by companies and professionals. In addition to a suit, shirt, accessories they also give mentoring, interview coaching and general guidance to give the best possible chance of making that great first impression to secure the role.

Smart Works began in 2013 – www.smartworks.org.uk

With two offices in London – West and North, one each in Edinburgh, Manchester, Reading, Birmingham, Newcastle and Leeds making their offering accessible throughout the UK. They offer the same services as Suited and Booted above. In addition, if successful and the role is secured, Smart Works will undertake a second meeting where a capsule starter wardrobe is given which could be five inter-changeable pieces including bags and shoes.

Either contact the organisation direct for more information or ask your local JobCentre Plus to refer you.

Whether you are having a virtual or face-to-face interview, this is your time to shine. You've done amazing to get through the process to this stage so make it count. Showcase your transferable skills. Remember, the employer is seeking enthusiasm to learn and commitment to their company not necessarily experience. Any employer will train but they can't train you to be enthused!

WORKPLACE SCENARIOS – WHAT WOULD YOU DO?

The following are real life experiences. What would you do if you were the person involved? Note down your thoughts on each scenario and check them against the answers on page 97

Case study 1

You like your own company. Your employer is having a BBQ in the grounds of their warehouse where you work as a porter. Your role entails all duties in the warehouse. You joined at the same time as four others who work in different departments upstairs. As the five of you are new to the company, your employer gives you all an early finish to go home and change before the BBQ later. You choose not to return but don't tell anyone. Afterall, they won't miss you.

On returning to work the following day, you are asked to clean-up the BBQ and store it at the back of the warehouse. You refuse as you didn't attend the BBQ you don't see why you should clean it.

Was that the right action?
Was there something else you could have done?

Case study 2

With a love of cooking, you secure your dream job in a corporate kitchen where your employer is going to send you for formal training at their cost. There's a huge amount of potential for your career. One of your new ideas for as dessert were incorporated to last week's menu giving great feedback.

The manager wants you to speak at his corporate client's meeting on how your journey is going. This is out of your comfort zone. You don't like public speaking.

What do you say?
Why?

Case study 3

After three years spent unemployed, you are selected for a training opportunity which has a permanent job attached to it. You are the eldest living at home. Your mum has five other children including a two year old. To your knowledge, she has never worked bringing you all up as a single parent has left her with little support, a diagnosis of depression and medication. She relies on you and wants you to stay at home to help her.

What goes through your mind?
What can you do?

Case study 4

It's the third week in your new job – which you love. However, you sense a chill in the air whenever Sarah, your Supervisor, is nearby. During the first week, there was a team chat on politics. You and Sarah completely disagreed. Things got a little heated. There's been a 'chill' since this.

What can you do?
What are the consequences of doing nothing?

Case study 5

You work in a busy office in the heart of the City. It's a new role – just your first week! Your manager gives you several tasks to complete before lunch. They will be in meetings but you have their mobile number.

The Supervisor asks you to come and help the distribution team unload a delivery which is blocking the road outside. The team there is understaff due to sickness and traffic is backing up. The manager's mobile is on answerphone. If you have the distribution team out, you won't complete your tasks.

What do you do?
Why?

Case study 6

It's your third day in your new job. Everything has gone wrong. The alarm didn't go off. Rushing around you didn't eat breakfast and picked up yesterday's top. Despite chasing the bus, you missed it. Now you are going to be late. Sweating, uncomfortable and embarrassed you finally arrive just 15 minutes late.

The manager is not impressed.
What could you have done to avoid this situation?

Case study 7

It's the day of your appraisal. Your manager hasn't been around much but you are confident it will go well. The manager raises two performance issues with you. The first was arriving late on site. The second was returning late from lunch. This is a shock to you. Afterall you had called ahead and spoke to the team when you knew you would be late due to traffic and Sue in the team saw you go to help a senior manager who had dropped some files making you late returning from lunch. Surely these messages had been passed on? You start to get upset.

What do you say?
What could you consider doing going forward to avoid this again?

COMMUNICATION

'Think before you speak'. How many times did you hear that as a child? Thoughtless communication causes damage – sometimes irreparable – in personal and work relationships. So that piece of advice can be crucial.

Oxford University has a couple of definitions on communication. The first is, '*imparting or exchanging information by speaking, writing or using some other medium*'. Sounds reasonable doesn't it? If we are giving information, we must think about the language we use, audience receiving that information, clarity, pace etc. The second definition is a little shorter '*means of sending or receiving information such as phone lines or computers*'. This refers more to the methods used.

It makes sense to 'think before we speak' to ensure the best chance of sharing that information effectively. However, there is much more to effective communication.

Effective communication takes more effort and no one teaches us how to do it. Education has a set curriculum to deliver, but if they churn out people who know a subject but not how to convey it whose fault is that?

Do parents know all the different points involved in effective communication to teach their children? Whilst most of us have heard 'think before you speak' fewer may know nothing about conflict management, assertiveness, body language, volume, pace, enunciation etc. Its no wonder there is so much angst and trouble in our lives and the world if we have no idea how to communicate effectively nor how to prepare for conversations.

The following are things I've learned over the years that have helped me in so many ways. I hope they help you too.

Key to successful communication, regardless of what method you choose to use or what the situation is - **preparation** is critical.

Preparing your communication: Think about what you want to achieve. Knowing your goal/purpose in delivering this communication helps you prepare the content. How might it be received? What might be the reactions to what you are going to say? Where are you going to say it? Can you say it a better way? Do you actually need to say anything at all? What is the best way of communicating in this instance? Face-to-face? Letter? E-mail? Text? Mobile?

Some key elements to consider:

Speaking – *Content* – have you done your research and got your facts right? *Tone* – what is the emotion you want to convey in this setting? Be prepared to listen and reflect back to agree next action points if they are needed. What about the environment? Does the setting need to be neutral, private or something else? Do you have the time to start this conversation now? Thinking about what you want to say, what could be the potential responses? How would you handle these? Do you need any signposting handy?

Listening – we have two ears and one mouth for a reason! Actively listen is a strongly desired attribute but needs practice in our technological society. Distractions are easy. Focus on what the individual says and reflect back (repeat it back to them in your own words to show you've understood or get clarity if you haven't). English is a hard language. Many words have similar sounds but different meanings especially where English is not a first language. Always reflect back. This shows you have listened and enables them to correct/clarify anything you haven't.

Writing – whether it's a letter, text or email, this method gives the writer time to read what they've written enabling edits before the reader receives it. Whilst you can't see the body language of the recipient you can make sure you've written something the best way possible before sending it. What is the tone of your message? What is the potential response? Do you need to send this?

Body Language is a key communication tool which can be effective in judging if someone has understood us, what emotions they may be feeling or if they are completely disengaged. We know body language is the biggest percentage of communication far bigger than tone and words. Remember, our habits are automatic. If we chew our nails, play with our hair, have our hands on our hips or something else, others can be judging us based on their perception. So be careful of your habits! Remember, poor body language is detectable over the phone as well. The listener can tell if you are slouching and disinterested.

Smile – the most effective tool in communication. You don't have to know everyone's name to engage with them. Engaging someone by stopping, to say hello and smiling is the foundation to grow great relationships. This also comes across in the lightness of your voice over the telephone.

Remember, for every action there is an equal reaction. With planning we can deliver the best possible action and mitigate its potential reaction.

When thinking of the tools to convey our communication, it's helpful to be, mindful of the industry accepted percentages of the areas that comprise communication:

Words make up 7% of communication

Your tone – 38%

Non-verbal communication (body language) is the largest element at 55%

It's interesting to note in the UK we spend the following times learning and using communication skills:

Mode	Years of training	Percentage of time used
Writing	12	9%
Reading	6-8	16%
Speaking	1-2	30%
Listening	0-0.5	45%

Clearly, we all need to up our listening skills training!

Some additional areas to think about when communicating:

Volume – are you loud enough to be heard by everyone but not so loud you are disturbing others or perceived as being aggressive?   It's key to bear in mind who we are talking to, what is the environment and what is the content.

Enunciation – clarity. How clearly are you talking? Mumbling never helped anyone understand anything. Are you being clear in what you are saying and is what you are saying flowing?

Pace – imagine listening to a favourite piece of music at an ultra-slow speed. Or ultra-fast. What would the affect be on you? Again, pace is a balance. Not too slow nor too fast.

Tone – happy, sad, angry, informative, condescending, helpful, enthused, positive, encouraging**.** We can prepare our words, content, method of communication, audience etc but if we get the tone wrong, we can have the opposite impact to the one we planned and prepared for.

Common Ground – connecting with someone you are communicating with and building a common ground is critical in effective, long-term relationships. Check out Barack Obama's inaugural speech on YouTube in 2004. At the time he was a little known Governor and qualified lawyer. You know the rest! The way he weaved connections with people he didn't know whose backgrounds on paper were completely different to his was a master stroke we can all learn from.

CONFLICT

How often have we all faced conflict and not actually known what to do? First, we have to know what type of conflict we're facing/potentially facing!

Actual – it's already happened. Think transport strikes. The only way to resolve this is talking and reaching a compromise agreement which best meets both side's needs.

Anticipated – we can see a potential issue which can cause conflict. We can usually take action to avoid the conflict.

Perceived – probably the most common form of conflict. When we think someone has done something to us. Think being cut up in the car whilst driving. The natural reaction is to become aggressive. We may swear, flash our lights, honk our horn or try to put the pedal to the floor and chase after them! Yet, we have no idea if they have someone in their car they need to get to the hospital. *We judge people on their actions not their intentions. But judge ourselves on our intentions without thinking of how others see our actions!*

Some top tips to manage conflict:

- Check your perception is fact! What evidence to you have your view to the situation is correct? You may need to have a conversation first.

- Take a moment to reflect on the situation – in the heat of the moment we can reach the wrong conclusion and cause an issue where there was none.

- When having a conversation – especially in a potential conflict situation – choose your communication technique to show you clearly disagree on the *issue* not the *individual*.

ASSERTIVENESS – what does it mean to you?

There are three levels of assertiveness:

Passive – someone who puts everyone else's needs above their own. Passiveness leads to low self-esteem and is often the reason people find themselves trapped in bad relationships and or jobs.

Assertive – balances others' needs as well as their own. Someone will often be in leadership/decision making roles whilst nurturing those around them.

Aggressive – puts their own needs above others, possible narcissist nature.

Take some time to think where you are.

Which of the three levels sums you up?

Why – what evidence do you have to think that way?

Are you happy with where you are – if not, what can you change?

NETWORKING

This is the best way of securing the quickest path to where you want to be, whether it's a particular job, education/training or something else. Like communication, networking is never taught. It's like one of those essential skills we think just descends on us when we need it! Sadly no. There are a number of techniques we need to engage with.

Networking sounds technical. It's just communicating with someone in person face-to-face or online. Six degrees of separation is the idea everyone is six or fewer social connections away from each other. I'm not sure if that's totally accurate but it is a very small world!

For me, there are different types of networks. Those built on relationships made through common ground as in people we've worked with or shared interests in – where we have a physical connection with them. In short, we've actually met them and know them to some extent. Some will be acquaintances. Some will be trusted contacts where there has been a mutually beneficial connection. These types of networks are easy to build on and can be long lasting through different roles changes. The connection with the person is more important than the position they hold.

Another type of network is, in my view, less valuable. These are largely networks built through platforms like Facebook and LinkedIn where there is no in person connection. On Facebook we can have huge numbers of 'friends' who we've never met, know little about and would likely be unreliable in a crisis. Are they really friends?

Whilst originally a business platform, LinkedIn has morphed into a professional version of Facebook. "Friends' on Facebook are equal to 'Connections' on LinkedIn. The mushroom effect of connections within our Linkedin network means we can have hundreds of connections but how many do we know directly? How many have we actually met? Who would really help us if we reached out? In my experience the connections I have with people I've personally met or worked with have proved more fruitful over the years compared to those connections on social media who just want to sell me something and only grow their own business. There is little mutual business benefit with faceless connections.

A network without relationships can be a fruitless empty shell. Looks good on the outside but there is no substance there.

A key mistake many people make is focussing on someone's position rather than the individual themselves. They let their connection to them drop when the individual leaves their role and focuses instead on their replacement. Yet the individual moving on can be one of their best contacts in a later role. Keeping physical contacts going is key to personal integrity and growth.

There is a famous story on leadership recounted by Simon Sinek called 'We only deserve a Styrofoam cup' about a former Under Secretary of State invited to speak at an event and how differently he was treated when he was invited to return to the same event a year later, by which time he had retired from his post. This illustrates the point above perfectly. I urge you to take the time to check the feature out on YouTube.

Another mistake many of us make is deciding whether people will be useful to us or not based solely on our assumptions of what their job title entails. Without having a conversation and building a network we could be missing out on a great connection with them directly or someone they know.

Once you have started your network, you need to grow it – keep talking, sharing ideas, go to mutual events etc.

Employer/trade events can unleash fear in people. Preparation will alleviate this. As the saying goes – face the fear and do it anyway!

Do your homework – who is going to be there? Make a point of noting any key contacts you want to make.

Your approach – body language, eye contact, what are you going to say? How are you going to interrupt if they are talking to someone else?

Some sample things I've used:

'Hi, I'm…… from……… it's my first time here – how about you?' No one is going to blank you at a networking event – the whole purpose is to get people talking and connecting. So don't hesitate to speak up.

People love talking about themselves. The more they talk the more you get to know about them, their work and connections – knowledge is power! So questions like…

'What are you involved with at the moment that really excites you?'

Make a mental note of contacts you want to follow-up. Of course, it's no good at all having someone's contact details and not contacting them! Use the tools discussed previously to catapult you to picking up your mobile. It could be the best call you'll make but you won't know until you try.

Never blank someone who comes to talk to you – again you don't know who they know!

What happens if you get stuck with someone you don't want to spend any more time with? Don't make the mistake of excusing yourself to use the bathroom – they could be waiting for you to come out! Instead be diplomatic – you never know this person could be your boss at some point in the future.

If you find yourself in a similar position, consider saying something like ….

'It's been lovely meeting you but I had a target of meeting three new contacts from this event. I am going to leave you now to continue networking and let you do the same'.

BE THE BEST VERSION OF YOU

Lao Tzu, a Chinese philosopher said 'if you are depressed, you are living in the past. If you are anxious you are living in the future. If you are at peace, you are living in the present'.

Take a moment to reflect on that statement. Do you agree with Lao Tzu?

Building a strong, resilient mind is key. There is no health without good mental health. Many well-trained sports people have experienced poor mental health despite having a strong physical body.

Building a strong resilient mind!

The more resilience we have, the easier it is to deal with the pressure of life, work and relationships. Starting to build a resilient mind is hard because self-belief/confidence is often missing. Therefore, faking it and a few key techniques are essential to change our behaviour and grow our self-esteem and therefore, resilience.

Now I'll share how I started to build my self-resilience.

Looking back now, it's as though I'm looking through the lens of someone else. I have learned to love, respect and value myself over the years. It has not been an instant journey. I know some of you reading this may still be in a toxic environment, feeling like you are in quicksand and cannot move forward. You may not feel you have the strength nor the courage to do so. **You do**.

At the time, my self-esteem, confidence and belief were non-existent. Coupled with the fact the ex-marital home was opposite the business we'd built up over the years. There was no escape. There was no respite.

For three years after we'd split, I would be in the marital home with the children directly opposite the shop we'd run. The house was a terraced two up two down with a narrow pavement adjacent to the busy main road. His girlfriend would endeavour to park her car on the pavement directly outside our front door.

At the time I felt desperately lonely, sad, weak, angry all at the same time. Looking back, I realise just how vulnerable she felt. When they split five years later, she wrote me a long letter wanting to be my friend! The constant focus I had was my two children then both under six looking to me for answers and a wider family that would not let me crumble.

'Never step outside without looking your best, your make-up on and your head held high. Never let them see they've got to you' my Great Aunt Olive – then over 80. Sound advice I still follow today and pass on to those I'm mentoring. When you look your best, your confidence naturally rises. Olive lived to 94. I never saw her without her full make-up and hair done with an immaculate, brightly coloured dress. She was always happy and

interested in others. I believe this was because she was so confident in herself and the reason she lived so long. So I follow and endorse her advice.

Affirmations are positive food for our brain. Quick shots of positivity on our strength, courage etc. I had many that I would repeat over and over. Things like 'I am strong', 'I am worthy' 'I will rise up'. At the time, the Court had ordered the sale of the ex-marital home but it hadn't been sold. So I wrote my affirmations on the walls around the house! I don't advocate that for you but maybe make a series of posters and put them up somewhere prominent in each room where you see them often. Positivity spreads as easily as negativity and self-doubt. Try it.

However, for those who are living with anxiety and depression they may need to consider a few more steps prior to reaching the affirmation stage. Acceptance and Commitment Therapy (ACT). Dr Steven Haynes devised ACT believing we fear what we care about. *If we avoid our fears, we are avoiding what we care about'*. Reflect on this statement – does it ring true to you? It does for me when I think of times I've given a speech in public or met a new client. We absolutely need to face our fears to move forward.

The key steps in Dr Haynes ACT are:

1. Accept what you can't control and stop focussing on it
2. Step back from negative thoughts
3. Focus on the present
4. Remove/ignore limiting self-definitions
5. Live by your core values
6. Take action to what matters

An interesting exercise to illustrate ACT is:

Do the opposite to what your negative thoughts tell you – shows your mind you can do it.

Example: whilst sitting down, tell yourself over and over you can't stand up. Then stand-up! Remember – negative thoughts only rule your life if you let them.

Dealing with intrusive thoughts

Most people have recurring negative thoughts. Most won't admit they do. Most hide these moments well. Intrusive thoughts are a natural part of being human. Acknowledging them, then dismissing them to focus on the positive task/thought is a key teaching of mindfulness. However, for some these thoughts can be so loud and overwhelming they prevent someone from moving forward.

Disagreeing with our minds can be tough. But what if we name our mind and then we're disagreeing with a name? Another idea from Dr Haynes which makes sense. Eg Person A has a recurring negative thought stopping them applying for a promotion at work because their negative mind is kicking in.

Person A names their brain Z. Anytime the negative though intrudes, Person A says 'I disagree with you Z, I'm applying now'. Sounds simple – it is and it works for many.

An alternative to naming your brain is put the negative thought into a song – it loses its power very quickly. Try it yourself. Put the negative thought to the tune of something like Happy Birthday.

'Fake it until you make it, until you become it', Dr Amy Cuddy

Check Amy's videos out online. In short, she was an exceptional student on top flight to academia had a bad car accident at 19 which, on first sight, wiped out all academic plans. On her long journey back to health and education, she termed the mantra 'fake it until you make it until you become it'. In short, no matter how scared you are, take a deep breath and one foot forward. Rarely does anyone other than you see an imposter. Gradually, your confidence grows and you become the person you want to be.

A key tool Dr Cuddy teaches is the Power Stand – easy to do and has scientific evidence to back up its effectiveness. You stand upright with your feet hip width apart and then put your hands either on your hips or above your head. Keeping your head upright and looking straight ahead, set a timer for 2 minutes (might want to set-up a timer on your mobile prior to getting into position!). To make it more powerful, breath in conscious cycles – breath in deeply for a count of three, hold your breath for a count of three and release the breath slowly for a count of three.

Scientific tests from saliva swabs taken before and after this exercise show a decrease in anxiety causing hormones – cortisol and adrenaline – and in increase in testosterone – a natural counterbalance to these hormones.

Fear is caused by our mind's natural process to keep us safe. When it perceives danger it floods our body with adrenaline and cortisol to give us all those awful symptoms of anxiety that makes us decide whether we are going to fight, flight or freeze in a given situation.

It's worth noting here that symptoms of anxiety are exactly the same as excitement. Think theme parks white knuckle rides. What do you feel queueing up to go on one of these rides? Racing heart, sweaty palms, dry mouth and so on? That's anxiety too. For many, anxiety is natural when related to events. Think coming home alone late at night, walking down a dark street to your front door. Once inside, you start to feel ok. For those living with anxiety disorder those symptoms are related to their emotions and do not end.

Making changes in our lives will involve having to make conversations with people outside our comfort zone. We all know what we need to do to get to where we want to be. We naturally lack the 'how to do it'. This comes back to the power of our mind in its mission to keep us safe. It will naturally flood our minds with 'what ifs' and procrastination (putting off doing things). Go back to my journey returning to employment after my marriage failed - remember single parent, two children under six, officially homeless and no official employment history for 10 years. With zero self-esteem I knew I had to go out and get a job. Shaking with fear inside I made a list of potential employers I could visit. I made a schedule of when I would go and see them. As soon as I woke up, I would immediately get up and get on with the schedule. This interrupted the mind's negative thinking cycle kicking in.

If you need to do something you don't want to do, don't think about it, just do it. Recently, I've discovered Mel Robbins who has made a fortune as a motivational speaker. You can find her on YouTube. She calls the process I used above her 5 second brain hack. Her method is when you wake up, count 5,4,3,2,1 and get up. A bit like the NASA space shuttle countdowns. We have just five seconds to take action before our procrastination part of our brain kicks in and we talk ourselves out of doing what we know we have to do. Try it next time you need to do something you don't want to do. It worked – and still works - for me.

Our brains are powerful tools. We have more capacity than we use. We can re-train our brain to think a different way. Depending on what we are going to do, we need to use the right part of our brain.

Pressure decisions. When we are put under pressure to give a quick answer it can often be the wrong answer. Pressure responses use our Neanderthal brain which is only concerned with the basics such as food, water and shelter. Considered responses bring in our Neocortex – the consequences part of our brain.

Example - If you see someone in danger in the sea, you don't way up the risks to jumping in to help, you steam straight in. Your Neanderthal brain takes over. This is the best chance of saving that person. However, if you are making a decision which will have a long time impact such as new area to live, you need to weigh up all the consequences using your Neocortex brain.

Some thoughts to consider to get to the best version of you:

1. Devise your plan of where you want to be, why and the steps you need to take to get there

2. Chris Gardener, the subject of In Pursuit of Happiness film shares some wisdom his mum gave him - 'the cavalry ain't coming – it's down to you'. Meaning you have to get on with your plan. No one can do it for you.

3. Have a 'what if' plan in place for vulnerable moments. Eg – if you are trying to drink less alcohol but know you often feel like a drink in the evenings – have some alternative non-alcoholic drinks or activities in place as a distraction.

4. Journal – write down your progress, small wins, reflect on your success, evaluate and change your plan as you go along

5. Change your mindset to think the way you want to be. Eg someone trying to stop smoking will often say 'thanks but I'm trying to stop' when offered a cigarette but a better response is to say 'thank you but I don't smoke'. It's a subtle difference but signals a shift in thought which will aid success.

6. Build in personal 'me' time. Taking time out for fun things such as exercise, drawing, sketching, thinking and just being is essential to everyone's wellbeing, more so when trying to make lasting changes in our lives. Self-care should be top of our priority list!

7. Who can help you in your quest? – a coach, a mentor?

NURTURE YOUR MIND AND SPIRIT

Our mind, body and spirit do not work in isolation. We'll look at mind and spirit here. Nurturing our bodies, we'll cover later.

We mentioned earlier that self-care should be top of our priority list. Afterall, 'you cannot pour from an empty cup'. If we don't look after ourselves – how can others rely on us? It doesn't matter what label we are wearing. Self-care doesn't have to cost a lot of, money or require a lot of space, time or equipment.

Checking in with ourselves on how we're feeling is a good starting point. We can use an app or pen and paper. Apps come down to personal choice with a variety on offer from gratitude journals to mood trackers – there is something for everyone.

Personally, I like to gauge where my mind is in a more basic fashion. The following are some tools I use on myself and on those I support.

Let's be realistic with the 0-10 scale used in these tools. Most of us don't score a continual '10'. We know we might be an 8 or 9 on most days. We may only score a 10 on passing our driving test, seeing a favourite band in concert or something similar event.

If we are scoring less than our usual 8 or 9, it's important to examine why? Are we consistently feeling lower than normal or is it just a bad day?

Is there part of our lives we are particularly anxious about? What can we do to improve our lower score and move closer to our usual score? Our place on any scale will move up and down depending on what's going on in our life and how well we are dealing with those issues.

Mood scale: Draw a line – horizontal or vertical, it doesn't matter. Give one end a score of '0' = very low mood. The other end score '10' = super happy. Mark where you are on the scale. The directional arrows just mark whether we are moving up or down. Everyone has 'off days' – think 'blue Mondays'. Continuous low score is a red flag to be aware off and address.

The colours are irrelevant – I just find colouring in soothing! You don't have to colour your tools in if you don't want to. They are effective either way. I've deliberately used my own drawings instead of polished photos to show effective tools are the ones you can replicate yourself with minimum cost quickly and easily.

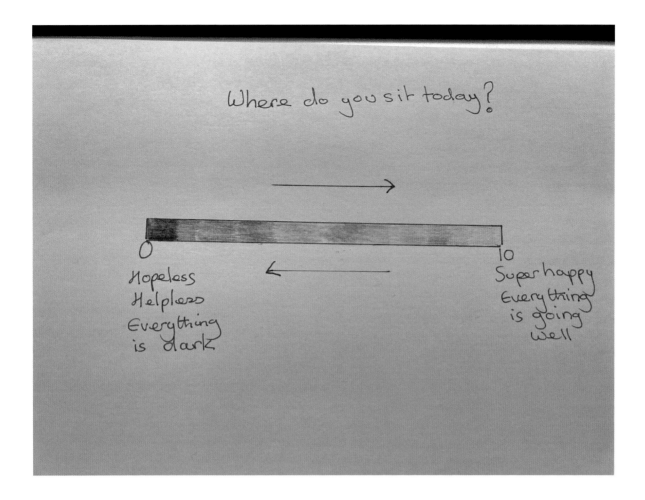

Face/emoji – Take a blank face outline and draw features to represent how you are feeling right now. You can use emojis on your mobile phone or mood cards the same way to illustrate how you are feeling. How long have you felt like this? Is it a one off?

Life circle – circles only work if they are of equal diameter all the way round. Just as we only function well if all areas of our life are thriving. Draw a circle using the 0 – 10 scale for each segment of your life. Example segments could be work, family, health, finances. It will soon become obvious what areas of your life need attention to stop you consciously or subconsciously worrying about them.

Example circles are shown below. The left side shows the ideal scenario where all areas of life score the optimum 10. However, the right side shows the reality where two areas score less than the full 10. These can indicate areas we may be worrying about.

Drawing our own life circle – which can have as many segments and classifications as we want – enables us to question what is going on in those areas that fall shorter than we'd like. In this example, are the reduced areas of relationships and finance about their own position or concerns they have in someone close to them? What can they do to increase these areas?

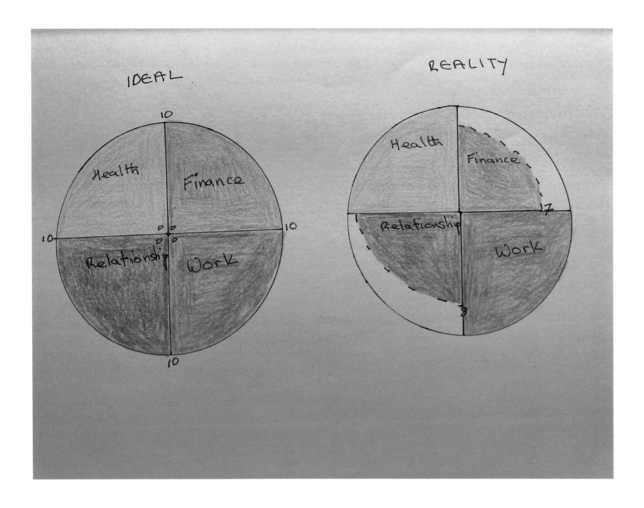

All of the three tools above identifies where our minds and spirits are currently, explore why and what would help us move up the scale.

Colours – different colours and hues have different meaning for people. Some find black comforting and stylish. Others find it dark, lonely and macabre. Thinking of our moods in terms of colours can ignite the investigation into why we feel that way and what we can do to improve our mood. All of these tools do the same job. You can use any of these or devise your own.

Self-care Toolbox

Anyone moving into their own home will have a toolkit for those minor repairs that need addressing. We can generally lay our hands on basic tools like a hammer, screwdriver etc. Waiting until we need these tools to put them together is a bad idea, costs us more time and money.

The same could be said for a self-care toolbox. Imagine a box you could lay your hands on easily that contained things that relax and calm you when you feel your emotions are rising? Few of us have such a box. We run through life on automatic pilot without a thought of our own nurturing and self-care. Those with insight have compiled such a self-care toolbox and use it daily. Everyone's selfcare toolkit will be unique. If might contain a doodle pad, colouring book, music, book of poetry, distraction tools, essential oils, affirmations. Building in some non-negotiable time for you each day for your selfcare builds resilience enabling you to deal with whatever life throws at you better as well as supporting those around you better too.

It takes three weeks of routinely doing selfcare activities before they become an automatic habit that we do without even thinking about it.

A box diagram detailing tools for nurturing our mind, body and spirit will give clarity on cross over tools which nurture more than one area making the selection of tools easier to identify and desired results of resilience and empowerment more achievable. Below are my box diagrams. I feel, for me, all of the tools are useful in all areas.

Mindfulness.   Breathing Apps.   Powerstand. Grounding tasks. Wellbeing training.
Sleep. Hydration. Nutrition.

MIND

Connections. Try something different. Goal setting. Purpose. Step outside comfort zone. Journaling. Gratitude diary.

Mindfulness.   Breathing Apps.   Powerstand. Grounding tasks. Wellbeing training.
Sleep. Hydration. Nutrition.

SPIRIT

Connections. Try something different. Goal setting. Purpose. Step outside comfort zone. Journaling. Gratitude diary.

Mindfulness.   Breathing Apps.   Powerstand. Grounding tasks. Wellbeing training.
Sleep. Hydration. Nutrition.

BODY

Connections. Try something different. Goal setting. Purpose. Step outside comfort zone. Journaling. Gratitude diary.

It's no good doing these box diagrams and building your self-care toolbox if you aren't going to put them into action. Nothing changes without change! So, build a schedule of when you can action your selfcare daily. Maybe your personal circumstance enables you to have a solid hour in the morning. For others, bite sized pieces of selfcare throughout the day work better. For me, what is most crucial is keeping the same time for your self-care. This makes it easier to turn this new routine into an automatic habit.

Stress is something we hear a lot of. Everyone is stressed. It's lost the impact it used to have on employers. For some people who have a stress disorder, hearing others use the word for everyday pressures is demeaning and doesn't help them get the help and support they need. Pressure is a much better term to use for stress experienced due to events. Once the event is over, the awful signs of stress dissipate. For those living with stress disorders, this is related to emotions and is much harder to deal with. For the sake of inclusion and clarity, it's really important to choose words carefully.

Let's take a closer look at stress. A perfectly natural process in every human being yet in its extremes it can render a person feeling absolute fear and helplessness. In the following we will look at what stress is and how we can control it rather than let it control us!

Reflecting back to the aftermath of my break-up, I now realise how stressed I was which led to periods of anxiety and depression – undiagnosed. At the time I was on automatic pilot and didn't realise what was happening to me. My first steps then in dealing with my feelings was what I now know as power breathing. The point of sharing this with you is to show if we aren't mindful of how we are feeling, stress can creep into our lives and take over without us even realising it.

So what is stress? The short answer is a safety mechanism. It's the body's way of keeping us safe – think fight, flight or freeze. It's job is to make us recognise we need to take action. Our brain will automatically release cortisol and adrenaline when it perceives a risk. It's these substances that cause the symptoms of stress/anxiety including sweating, racing heart rate/palpitations, unable to make a decision, unable to concentrate, an overriding fear, dry mouth etc. This enables us to make a decision – fight, flight or freeze depending on the situation.

Once the event is over, the levels of cortisol and adrenaline start to dissipate along with the symptoms. However, for someone who has a stress disorder these symptoms and feelings are constant likely requiring support and professional intervention.

Stress related to events are normal, natural and not harmful. However, a better term is 'pressure' as its event related. Stress related to emotions is harmful , constant and needs professional treatment and understanding which is why we need to choose our language clearly to ensure no one living with a stress disorder feels excluded.

Don't be fooled by anyone – especially in the workplace – saying a little stress is good for us as it focuses us to get things done. Stress is never good for us. A little 'pressure' might be and won't negatively affect anyone around who really does have a stress disorder. So challenge language used!

We've already looked at some quick and easy selfcare tools to examine where we are. Another is the stress bucket. This coupled with a series of questions is very effective at visually reducing the pressure we put on ourselves. This technique can also be used for scheduling work more efficiently or planning an event.

I first devised this whilst presenting to an organisation as part of the MHFA England team. The CEO, a national trainer and myself were presenting a bitesize introduction to mental health first aid to a room full of managers from the corporate consulting world.

The national trainer spoke about the mechanics of stress and how our mind is like a big container which has life and work events flowing into it. If we have strong resilience, we are able to deal with these events efficiently and not get overwhelmed. A bit like turning the tap on and letting some water flow out. However, if we don't have good resilience, more and more events will flow in, stress levels will rise and we become very unwell as our 'bucket' overflows.

Looking around the room I noticed expressions of bewilderment. The diagram the national trainer used was clear enough – a bucket with a tap at the bottom, events flowing in at the top. If the tap wasn't turned on regularly – i.e. events weren't faced and dealt with – the bucket would overflow. It needed to be more relatable on a personal level for the audience to absorb the mechanics.

Armed with a flipchart and pen, I drew another bucket this time divided up into sections containing things in my life that were on my mind at the time in no particular order. The idea was literally to empty everything on my mind at that time into the bucket. It went something like this:

Adult child's partner. There felt a distance between us. I had a conversation with them. Turns out they felt uneasy - they didn't know how to feel when around us. We now get on famously.

Management 8 page reports with graphs and stats that no one read. My work was reported to the Board. The standard management reports took too much time. I asked my manager if I could give her a bullet point list of my work that she could include in her management report. She agreed!

Working away from home – partner not happy with me being away – think Andrex puppy! My choices were leave the job, leave the partner or accept my partner's moaning for a few days before/after each trip and keep the job I loved. I chose the latter. Acceptance was all I needed to do to reduce the pressure here.

Social Media - Company website, company intranet, company CSR and general marketing pieces. Took too much time! I asked a colleague, who knew my work and loved social media, would they agree to take this over. They said Yes! Getting their help reduced the pressure here by 80%.

The black text represented each thing that was on my mind. It was a little worrying at this point as not only was the expressions of bewilderment in the audience – they were now on the CEO's and National Trainer's faces too! Remember, this wasn't planned nor rehearsed. I was going completely off script. I kept going. "once you've completed your stress bucket ask yourself these questions:

1. What can I not change and need to accept?
2. Who can help me?
3. Is there a better way of doing something?
4. Are my feelings correct – what evidence do I have for feeling this way?

As you ask and answer these questions against the items in your stress bucket, your mind sees and accepts the real situation and those feelings of stress reduce." I have written each answer in red so you can see how the system works. Try it yourself.

Glancing around the audience expressions of 'oh I get it – that makes sense' replaced the looks of bewilderment – including those of the CEO and national trainer! I was invited to join the Board following this and the stress bucket template and questions became part of the Adult course at that point – although termed a stress container.

Stress breeds self doubt which stops us moving forward. Some top tips for when these feelings occur:

Mantra: Use your mantra!

Power Breathing: Doubts can quickly grow. Learning to control your breathing will regulate your blood flow and calm the symptoms:

- Breathe in deep and evenly for a steady count of three
- Hold your breath for a steady count of three
- Breathe out slowly for a steady count of three
- Repeat this several times until the feelings subside.

There are many free breathing gifs you can find on Google which give you a visual pattern to follow as well as breathing in a measured way similar to the above.

Visualisation: Think of your 'happy place' and focus on all your senses. What do you hear, see, taste and feel? Example: a tropical beach, where you **feel** the warm sun and sand, **hear** the lapping sea and barbeque crackling, **taste** the peach juice beside you, **see** the blue sky. Visualisation works best when you are alone and can concentrate on your happy place and all the senses you connect with it without any distractions.

Plan: any projects/events. Including what could go wrong, what could you do about it? If you think of all bases, the fear of failing will reduce because you have prepared.

Get help: if after all of the above, you still feel the doubt – ask for help. It's a strength not a weakness.

Do something different

Work and home can quickly become routine. It's important to keep both fresh and not do everything on routine automatic pilot. I remember many periods when I had a strong feeling of 'I want to go home'. No idea what 'home' meant other than a place away from all the problems of life to recharge my batteries. During these times I was not mindful of my own wellbeing. More importantly I didn't notice life was literally passing me by. I didn't take the time to notice the beauty around me. Consequently, I was always exhausted, running on empty and we all know you can't pour from an empty cup!

We have to force ourselves to do things differently. To build in some nurturing elements to our daily life and enjoy it not waste it. It takes courage and strength to put ourselves first but by doing so we are energised and more available to those that need us.

Finding what works for you is key. Some things you could consider:

1. Practice mindfulness – take notice of where you are and really focus on one thing
2. Listen to a different type of music on your headphones – concentrate on the words/tune
3. Take a sketch pad and draw a scene – it doesn't have to be a masterpiece
4. Start a journal – make notes each day of what's happened, how you feel, what you've learned and what you are grateful for
5. Check out local things to try both at home and work for during your lunch breaks.
6. Start your own vlog or blog
7. Can you do something online?

Have you heard the expression 'what goes on at work goes home with you and vice versa'? A lot of the time this is because there is no visible gap between the two.

Instead try getting 'in the zone' before entering your place of work and change the zone to home at the end of the day.

Confused?

Let's take it a step at a time. Before entering your place of work, try taking a few minutes to think about the day ahead. Visualise the environment and team. When you go into the building take a few minutes to check your appearance, maybe do some power breathing with a gif you downloaded. By doing this you switch from home to work mode more easily.

Once you complete your journey home after work, take a few minutes before going in to think about the evening ahead. What are you looking forward to doing? Instead of just slumping in front of the tv – which makes the evening go really quick – can you try out something new? Maybe something from the ideas above? Are there any courses/clubs/choirs locally or online you can try?

When you start investigating, it's amazing how many free events and places there are locally from art galleries to museums to music and theatre events – something for everyone, but you have to seek and find.

The more variety we give our minds the healthier and more productive we will be.

WHO'S REALLY GOT YOUR BACK?

A harsh lesson to learn in life is people you trust aren't always worthy of that trust. Negativity and positivity spread like an out of control wildfire. If we surround ourselves with the wrong people, we can soon find ourselves in a bad situation.

Throughout my life I've had to remove people, including family members, who didn't have my best interests at heart. You have to be ruthless in this to be healthy and able to be there for others.

A simple evaluation table can highlight where you might have potential issues. The short example below shows Sue might need replacing :

Name	What support do they give?	Rating – 1 = awful, 5 = great
Sue	Emotional – my friend since childhood	2 – I overheard her talking about me
Dave	Manager at work	5 – encouraging, listens to me

Make the time to look at those closest to you at home and at work. Who supports and encourages you? Who maybe not so good for you? Who's always negative and drags you down?

Organisations within the field of mental health and well-being all advocate the same 5 Ways to *Enhance Your Well-being*:

Connect – call/meet someone you haven't seen in a while
Give to others – do something – no matter how small – for someone else
Be active – exercise releases endorphins and makes us feel great
Keep learning – our brains are active. If they aren't fed, they will start going dormant
Take notice – make yourself look at and concentrate on nature when you are out and about

Follow an organisation that exudes positivity like Action for Happiness on Twitter. Lord Layard an economist wrote a book decades ago about the importance for an organisation's bottom line for their staff to be happy. So true, if only every employer had the same outlook! Action for Happiness will have positive posts to inspire you. Check them out – www.actionforhappiness.org.

KINDNESS

Includes being kind to yourself – not just being king to others. Costs nothing but what a difference it makes! Taking the time to stop and think about a situation brings clarity and prevents making it worse.

I used to always make assumptions without questioning what evidence I had to feel that way. It always made situations worse. Here are a few things that have helped me be kinder – to myself and others.

Don't immediately think you know why someone is behaving in a certain way. There can be multiple reasons. Why not ask them before jumping to conclusions? We judge others on their actions not their intentions, because we don't know what their intentions are without asking them – we just make assumptions.

The stress we put on ourselves in 'thinking' we've upset someone else or done something wrong is often resolved by speaking with them. Never assume anything. Always ask – but remember your tone, environment, body language and words you use. In other words – prepare what, where and how you are going to speak with them and be prepared for anything they say. You may well have upset them but by asking them, you get the opportunity to put things right and repair the relationship.

Equally, if someone has said something which upsets you, discuss it with them. Don't assume they meant it in the way you have taken it.

The wolves – self doubt

There is an old American Indian saying concerning wolfs. It's said there are two wolfs inside each of us. One is self-worth and full of love the other is self-doubt full of intrusive negative thoughts. The one that survives is the one you 'feed'. Check the video our on YouTube – haunting background music!

Remember this next time you doubt yourself and feed the self-belief wolf in you by re-affirming how great you are. Remember fake it until you make it until you become it. Your resilience and self-worth will grow exponentially over time.

Face your fear

The only way to deal with our fears is to face them. Ignoring them won't miraculously solve them! The more we suppress the fear the more problematic things will become. We have to deal with all issues that worry us to be whole and healthy. Facing your fear may involve difficult conversations – remember the tips earlier in this book.

At this point it's fitting to share an experience of mine. As a child, I remember my mum's fear of heights. She wouldn't even stand on a chair to change a lightbulb! This fear rubbed off on me. As an adult many years later whilst on holiday in Madeira, during a tour of the levadas, I was forced to confront my learned fear. You may know levadas are narrow waterways which travel up the hills. Fish are put in the water as an indicator of the water's freshness. It was a particularly misty this morning. The weather was calm. However, I wasn't when suddenly the mist cleared and I was standing on a 12 inch ledge over 4,500 feet up with a small wire fence between me and a big drop! The guide said I could either face my fear and climb down with the others or stay there. Of course, I faced my fear and climbed down before realising how irrational my fear was. It wasn't even my fear! Just something I learned from mum.   Since then, I've experienced some amazing sights and heights including the Burj Khalifa's viewing platform in Dubai – really high!

Banter – Be Aware

There is a fine line between banter and insult both in the workplace and in your personal life. Remember under legislation a third person who overhears something you said can complain leaving you open to disciplinary procedures. Think before you speak. What is it you want to say? how are you going to say it? Is there a kinder way to say it or words to use? How can it be interpreted? Is there a need to say anything at all?

In the workplace someone who is offended by something you said either directly to them or to a third party which they overheard can challenge you, your employer and, if you are a contractor on a client's site, the client as well under the Equalities Act 2010 free of charge at an Employment Tribunal. This process can go on years and cost thousands in legal feels not to mention mental pressure and reputation. There are nine protected characteristics under this Act. It's easy to be captured under its remit if you do not think before speaking or acting with dignity and respect.

Gossip!

Where there are human beings there are gossips – don't get involved. You will eventually be the subject of gossip if you do. Gossiping is one of the unkindest things humans can do to each other. Also check under toilet cubicle doors before speaking about something you don't want others to hear. Here's why I mention this….

In one of my first jobs as a teenager, there was an over-zealous supervisor with a curt manner. I was too young to consider she may be dealing with issues that made her curt. It never entered by head at the time to speak to her privately about her manner and impact on me. I was a 'know it all' teenager. During the break we were in the toilets and I was moaning about the 'cow' of a supervisor. You guessed it. A toilet flushed and out walked the same supervisor! I never went back after my shift such was my immature embarrassment. Now with mature eyes I would have done everything differently.

NURTURE YOUR BODY

Have you ever put diesel in a petrol car? No? luckily me neither but I've heard from others who have. The result is a car that doesn't go anywhere, stutters to a halt and costs a lot to put right.

The same can be said with putting the wrong fuel into our bodies. Overtime problems will accumulate, although we won't see the gradual changes going on inside – we'll just see the end damage.

Poor diet is down to poor choices. I know some readers may completely disagree with that and think it's down to poverty. For me, that's a cop out to excuse laziness. Speaking from my experience as a single parent who never had the security of benefits but had to feed and clothe myself and my children as well as pay all bills with a series of ad hoc jobs on very little income, we never ate fast/processed food continuously. These were just once in a while treats.

It's cheaper and more nutritional as well as educational and fun to cook from scratch with children. I found involving my children enabled them to explore new foods in turn opening up their food choices. This was the time I started buying bags of dried soya protein from health food shops – long before the popularity of plant food and brands like Quorn. Dried soya protein then was sold in health food shops in large, cheap bags. It was tasteless and needed a lot of herbs and spices. Experimenting with different combinations of flavours made it more fun.

Although my children are dedicated meat eaters, I remained a plant based fan and eat no meat. There are plenty of choices out there to accommodate every preference and plenty of books and on-line recipes. Tinned and frozen fruit and vegetables are just as healthy as fresh so don't worry if you can't get to the shops daily for fresh. There's always a solution!

Food really is cheap if we buy fresh and not convenience foods. Even more fun is growing your own veg. You don't have to have acres of garden to do this. A balcony, windowsill or pots in light areas indoors will work for growing herbs, tomatos etc. Aquaponics involves growing plants in water. Various kits are available on line from basic options to high end! There is a lot of information on different options for growing vegetables where lack of outdoor space is a consideration. Even something as quick and easy as egg and cress or kale shoots nurtures our soul. There is an option for everyone. What's yours?

www.nhs.uk has clear resources on food choices, the real facts about diets and how to stay fit and healthy. Check it out first as there is a lot of mis-information on social media, in our communities and amongst family and friends. Why listen to food information from anyone other than a qualified nutritionist? Take sugar free diet books. Look closely, they usually contain sugar under one of its different names – fructose, dextrose etc. When choosing processed foods – especially cheap ones – check the labels. Manufacturers often use two mediums for producing flavour in their products. These are fat or sugar.

Sugar, sweet, sweet sugar….

A key thing to remember is your sugar intake. Sometimes known as the 'silent killer', excess sugar along with poor diet of too much processed food can lead to things like Type 2 Diabetes – which can be reversed by changing our diet. Tough choices need to be made.

'No pain no gain'. I heard this on just about every exercise DVD of the 80s and 90s! But it is true. We have to put the effort in. To do so, we need some knowledge. The current recommendations for sugar intake is seven teaspoons per day for an adult. World Health Organisation wants to reduce this to 6. One teaspoon of sugar = 4gms.

Checking labels will reveal how much sugar is in each item empowering you to make the right choice. Be mindful of your sugar intake – much of which will be hidden – will improve your overall wellbeing.

Talking about labels

Food labelling is so important. Taking the time to see just what you are eating can help you understand why you feel sluggish, tired or energised. Every label lists the ingredient by quantity first. So, the packet of pork sausages you've picked up may have things like water, preservatives and cereal ahead of pork which is listed as little as 20% towards the end. Food items generally have a sell by and use by date. Manufactures have to put preservatives in to meet these dates. So, unless you buy fresh and make things yourself, you can be eating a shed load of nasty things of no nutritional value!

Food outlets can operate different labelling styles. The traffic light is the easiest to understand. Red – eat rarely. Amber – eat occasionally. Green – a good choice. Some though will use percentages which can be confusing. The best way of working out what you are eating is to look at the weight of the packet and then the 'per 100gms' columns. Using this system enables more accurate understanding of what you are eating. If the contents of the packet is 200gms and the 100gm column states, for example, 7% fat, you know you are having 14% fat if you eat all of the contents.

The British Heart Foundation has lots of free information you can download from their website including food labelling crib cards.

It takes time to change bad habits to good ones. Don't beat yourself up if you fall off your plan. The key is to get back to your plan quickly.

'I don't have time to make everything fresh' I hear your say

Procrastination allows all of us to put off making any changes. We literally talk ourselves out of doing what we know we should do.

We can all make changes no matter how busy we are. I remember getting my first fridge freezer when re-housed following our period of being officially homeless. It cost £120 out of Co-Op then in Eltham High Street – now a Primark I think! It took me 18 months to pay off. Juggling several part-time ad hoc jobs as well as two children at primary school, I had to find a way of eating cheaply, nutritionally whilst filling tummies up.

Armed with a freezer cook book – remember this was before the Internet! I started batch cooking. We would get all the ingredients to make multiple portions of 'ready cook meals! Currys, chillis, casseroles, stews, hotpots. You name it we made it. All we had to do during the week was take something out for dinner that night.   No preservatives, hygienically prepared, nutritional food and we had fun making it.

Why not get into the habit of batch cooking and freezing your favourite foods? Whether you have a family or not it occupies your mind, gets your creative juices flowing, is cheap and saves you so much time to enable you to get on with life!

Jack Monroe is an award winning food writer and poverty campaigner. She started writing blogs on how she fed herself and her child nutritionally on very little money. Check her recipes and books out at www.cookingonabootstrap.com for ideas.

Vitamins & minerals

With the amount of money in 'healthy living' it's no wonder we can be bombarded by thoughts that health and happiness lie in a specific diet or supplement. Celebrities have written books on sugar free diets – only to include sugar's different names - fructose, dextrose, sucrose, glucose etc!

Why do we waste our time and money on information not written by qualified nutritionists who have studied their craft for years?

Key points the nutritionists share on Growing Talent concerning vitamins and minerals are:

1. Eating a wide variety of colours of fruit and veg give a wide range of vitamins and minerals that the body can easily use.
2. Eating fresh fruit is better than drinking juice. The body breaks down the fruit differently once it's been juiced losing a lot of the good stuff like fibre, slow release sugar etc.
3. Taking too many supplements can have an overdosing affect. You may be taking what you don't need.
4. The only vitamin they recommend – which is one of the cheapest – is vitamin D due to the lack of sunshine in the UK. Sunshine is the key source of Vitamin D absorbed through the skin. Of course, care should be taking not to expose the skin to more than 15 minutes sunshine without protective sun cream.

H2O vs Caffine

Water is so under rated when we consider our health. It flushes our system of impurities, keeps us alert and stops us getting headaches through dehydration. Check your pee to see if you're dehydrated. The brighter it is, the more hydrated you are. If you find yourself feeling sluggish, with headaches and lack of concentration, drink some water. You will likely feel better. Hot water with a slice of lemon and/or root ginger in cleansing, refreshing and warming when it's cold.

Caffine often gets a bad press. For some who have a sensitivity to anxiety they will be advised not to have more than 300grms of caffeine a day. There are decaf products available. For everyone else, there is no harm in having a coffee and follow it with a glass of water. Labels must be read by those who have a sensitivity to anxiety as it is in so many everyday products such as cough medicine.

Many people say 'Caffeine has no effect on me. I drink coffee all day'. Is this the case or is it more likely they have built up a tolerance and wouldn't notice any issues until they stopped drinking coffee? Everyone is different.

Personally, I can drink coffee before going to bed and still sleep soundly. I can also go days without drinking any coffee nor experiencing any withdrawal symptoms.

It's important to remember we are all different.

LONELINESS OR ISOLATED – WHAT'S THE DIFFERENCE?

These might seem the same but there is a vast difference. Let's look at the official Oxford Dictionary definitions of each for clarity:

'Loneliness is a sadness because you have no friends or company'

'Isolation is being separated from'

In short, some people can live in isolation yet not be lonely. They are happy with their own company. Often their isolation is a lifestyle choice.

Loneliness is all encompassing for some people in different environments. We've all had the feeling of being alone even when in a crowded room. It's not a place people choose to be. It engulfs some without them even realising it leaving them numb to move forward, taking over their life.

It's important to be mindful of loneliness. If you feel it creeping in, examine if you often feel like this? Do you feel like this in particular situations or around particular people?

The global pandemic evidenced an explosion in loneliness amongst people of all ages from all cultures and social background. Loneliness is a human condition which knows no boundaries.

Lockdown saw a spotlight put on loneliness and how it can ultimately be a killer. There are things we can do to arrest loneliness. Some examples below:

- Build self-esteem to give confidence to connect with others
- Join others to explore mutual interests – maybe try out new ones
- Support others who are feeling lonely – focussing on others needs dampens the impact of our own loneliness
- Do something outdoors with a neighbour/friend
- Learn something new

Lockdown, due to the global pandemic, has forced many constraints on our liberty. However, we can still reduce the impact of loneliness through innovation. Let's take each of the points above and put them into a lockdown setting:

- Build self-esteem – devising and using our mantra, affirmation, selfcare tools routinely until they become an automatic habit. Utilise the 5,4,3,2,1 technique to override any natural procrastination. Consider adding in some on-line classes
- Devise a friend/family challenge on art, music, sketching, baking, cocktail making etc
- Support a friend or neighbour who is lonely – a daily socially distanced conversation, do some shopping for them, cook and deliver them a meal etc

- Do something outdoors with a neighbour/friend – download some nature checklists on birds, flowers, tress etc. Use these to see how many you spot in a local park/woodland. Sketch something you see with your eyes shut then open and see which version you prefer. Challenge each other to write a song or poem about the view.
- Learn something new – instead of getting a tradesperson in to do the decorating, tiling or similar job, why not use YouTube to see how it's done and try it yourself? Or investigate an online accredited course in something you've always wanted to do.

Being mindful of loneliness creeping into our lives enables us to offset it before it takes hold. There is always something we can do but urgent action is required before loneliness takes over.

PERSONAL FINANCE

Who teaches basic finance? Schools don't. Often parents don't. Employers don't either. Without this very basic skill we can get you into a lot of difficult situations.

I'm sharing a few basic things I've learned over the years here. Remember, I am not an Independent Financial Advisor so do your own investigations/research prior to making any decisions.

Direct Debits vs Standing Orders

I never knew there was a choice when payments are the same amount until I got burned by a direct debit. In my case I had several direct debits which I'd not paid any attention to. One had a roll-on clause which means if I didn't cancel by giving one month's notice prior to the annual anniversary I was tied in for another year and they could automatically increase the cost of the payment! Ultimately, I got this resolved by speaking with my bank and the company I had the direct debit with.

So what are the key differences?

Standing Order – you have control. No company can increase payments from your account without your authorisation. Ideal if you have something which costs exactly the same amount each month – think subscriptions.

Direct Debit is usually raised by a company providing you with services. The mandate (authorisation) you sign will show the amount due, date it will be taken – check the small print for roll-on clauses! Remember, the amounts they take can be varied so keep an eye on these.

It's always best to use Standing Orders where possible. Direct Debits are great in circumstances where you absolutely don't want to run out of the service – think insurance policies.

Whichever method you use, keep a regular check on your bank account. Many people discover they are still paying Direct Debits for services they ceased receiving long ago!

Bank accounts

Back in the day I opened my first bank account as a single parent. I just wanted a basic account – no frills and no service charges. The problem with some humans – me included – is no matter how much information and notifications banks give, there is a key failure point – in not reading it! So it was after a number of years I found my account switched to a service charge account with free mobile and travel insurance in exchange for a monthly fee. As my career progressed and I got busier I just deleted emails from the bank.   Luckily I noticed one stating the fee was increasing to £19.99 per month – over £200 per year for services I never used! A quick call to the back got me moved bank to my basic account with no service charges.

The point of illustrating this is to show how easy it is to 'lose' money just through being busy.

If you are going to use all the services you receive from your bank account and can't get them individually for a more efficient price, it might be worth paying a monthly fee to your bank. Everyone's personal circumstances are different. Don't just do what your family/friends do.

Round-up Accounts

It's a great way to save with little effort but be mindful not every bank offers this. The way it works is – when you buy something using your debit card, the bank will round it up to the amount you've asked the (£1, £5, £10 etc). The difference is moved to your round-up account. So, if you asked the bank to round up to the nearest £1 and buy something for £4.25, your bank will deduct £5 from your account putting 75p into your linked savings account. This doesn't sound much but it mounts up quickly. Over a year this can pay for something substantial like your holiday spending money!

Before looking at any new financial product, I always check out comparison websites like www.moneysupermarket.com or www.moneysavingexpert.com Apart from bank accounts, there's diverse information on all financial products.

Online banking

The majority of us now have online banking. It's quick, easy and accessible. However, there are a few things to bear in mind:

1. In some cases, your balance won't be live. Make sure you account for all payments you've made even if they aren't showing up.
2. Be mindful when paying someone on line. If you enter a wrong digit, the bank only has to use 'reasonable' effort to rectify the error
3. If the bank makes an error in a payment you've made – they have to reimburse you.

Regularly check your bank account. It's believed fraudsters will try taking a small amount from your account before a bigger amount. So check and query anything you aren't sure of.

Savings

It doesn't matter what money you have coming in, there is always a way to save. It's important to build a cushion of 3-6 months' salary for events that happen beyond our control. Using the comparison sites mentioned earlier will give a good overview of products out there to choose from.

A few things to consider. We've mentioned Round-up accounts already. You can set up multiple bank accounts and move your money from your current account into long term savings (rainy day) and one for large items like holidays. You will only see the money left in your current account and be less likely to over spend.

ISA's are a good option. Cash ISAs don't pay much interest but your money is safe. Stocks and Shares ISAs are a good way of increasing your return but only over the long-term. Shares can go down as well as up. You can also encounter funds being wound-up like the infamous Neil Woodford who lost billions of savers money yet didn't have his own resources affected.

I was one of Neil Woodford's investors. Luckily only invested a small amount. I made the investment based on Neil's reputation as the number one fund manager. Don't be fooled by reputations. Do your research. If you do invest in a Stocks and Shares ISA have a price in mind you want to achieve and pull out before it drops. The way I view stocks and shares now is the same as gambling. You should only gamble with anything you can afford to lose and don't chase losses.

Beware of the introductory offers for savings accounts. These are usually only open to new savers and are often time limited. Make sure you put a note in your diary a month before the time limit for expiry to decide whether to stay or move your money.

Remember with ISAs, the minute you draw the money out, it becomes taxable. If you want to move an ISA to another ISA with a more attractive interest rate, make sure you get a 'transfer-in' form first. Withdrawals count as part of your balance. Example: where the ISA limit is £20,000, you have £15K in your ISA and withdraw £3K the amount you can put back into your ISA is £5K not £8K.

Debt

So easy to get into. Sometimes a nightmare to get out of. Ignoring debt won't make it disappear. You need to take action. Never, ever pay for debt advice. You can get free, impartial professional help from:

www.moneyadviceservice.org.uk
www.stepchange.org
www.nationaldebtline.org

Methods of Payment

People will usually have three key methods of paying for goods and services although more options come on line regularly such as Apple Pay. We'll look at the three main ones:

Debit cards, credit cards or cash

Each has an edge over the others depending on what the situation is.

Debit Cards

Most people use these for everyday expenses. Easy to carry and only the exact amount you spend leaves your bank account. However, they are easy to overspend on! Especially if using Tap and Go. Be mindful – especially on a night out!

Cash

Is useful in haggling for discounts on large goods. It can also stop you over spending on a night out. However, once cash is drawn out of bank accounts, any unspent money is rarely paid back in! Cash is also irreplaceable if lost!

Credit Cards

When used appropriately, Credit Cards can be the best method of payment. www. moneysupermarket.com explains how. 'In 1974, the government reformed the law concerning consumer credit. Under Section 75 of the Consumer Credit Act, credit cards must provide protection for purchases above £100 and below £30,000.' So for large items in this price bracket, your credit card provider can help you get your money back if the following happen:

- You buy an item that's faulty or damaged and you can't get a refund or replacement through the retailer or trader

- Your item arrives and it isn't the same as the description

- Your item isn't delivered but you've still been charged

- The retailer or trader goes out of business before you've got your item.

If you encounter any of these issues speak with the retailer or trader first. If the issue isn't resolved, then speak with your credit card provider.

As advised by www.moneysupermarket. com, you won't be covered in the following circumstances:

- The item costs less than £100 or more than £30,000

- The item is technically two transactions – for example, two single train tickets costing £60 each, so £120 in total

- You use a store card

- You use a third party payment provider to pay or to book

Third party payment providers like PayPal will offer their own payment protection scheme, and third party holiday providers should come with specific holiday protection.

Loans

Before reaching for a store card or payday loan – ask yourself do you really need that item now? Can you save for it? Can you find a way to get extra money in maybe a second job or turning your hobby into a paid for service for others to use? So often we shop on impulse without thinking it through. Once you enter into a loan agreement you are going to be in a cycle of having less money each month making the payments – not to mention any interest!

Mortgages

Some people are unaware of the Bank of England's base rates have anything to do with getting a mortgage. Which is probably why some people get mortgages they can ill afford.

The way it works, is a mortgage product will have an interest rate which you are tied into for a set amount of time. There are various mortgage products. Two of the key ones are a tracker – where the rate will fluctuate depending on the Bank of England's base rate and a fixed rate – the interest is fixed regardless of whether the Bank of England's interest rate goes up or down.

So if the Bank of England's rate is 0.25% and your mortgage company's is 3.5% you will pay 3.75% every month. Make sure you can afford your repayments easily to cover future increases in fares, living costs and unforeseen problems.

The Bank of England's interest rate used to impact savings but few savings accounts have any interest rates attached to them now!

It's always best to seek advice from a qualified Financial Adviser who is independent and can advise on all the products from all financial institutions to get you the best product. www.unbiased.co.uk and www.ifa-direct.com both have lists of independent, qualified advisors based on location.

Budgets

Budgets are an invaluable tool to keep on top of your finances. Key is to take the time to think about every outgoing you have over a year so you capture everything. You can then build in monthly payments to cover these via standing orders or direct debits. You can do this as a spreadsheet or in a notebook or use a budget app.

A word of warning on budget apps for those technically minded whose life is on your mobile. Any app which is linked to your bank account can be in breach of your bank's Terms and Conditions leaving you open to fraud. Always check with your bank first to make sure they approve. Many have their own apps.

SOCIAL MEDIA

Those of us of a certain age learned etiquette when face-to-face with friends, our socialising, at work which seems to have dissolved over the years with the introduction of social media and coffee shops!

Who would have thought just 10 years ago we would now not be able to walk down the street without trying to dodge people walking along texting, or avoiding people in the supermarket with their free coffee in one hand, texting on the other and somehow trying to manoeuvre an errant shopping trolley!

I've lost count of the times I've been in meetings with people who proudly place their mobile on the table as if to say 'you are just not that important to me'. These are the same people who don't make the most of networking. Prior to going into the meeting they have their heads down texting or updating their social media pages. What happened to building networks by talking to people around them?

Can you believe there is now a condition known as Digital Dementia? A warning to us all maybe.

It is now accepted and proven by evidence that using social media is addictive. When we get a 'like' or put a post-up that someone likes the feeling we get is almost euphoric and caused by the release of Dopamine – a neurotransmitter responsible for the reward and pleasure area of our brains. This feeling is addictive and is the same feeling from gambling – putting a bet on and when we win, and drinking alcohol – before becoming drunk. For more on this check out Simon Sinek on YouTube or a Google search.

Back in the day, social media platforms started employing Attention Engineers (yes, really) to instigate and grow this circle of anticipation. This practice originated in Las Vegas to keep people gambling – the 'magic of maybe'.

Standford University, USA published a report which measured the impact of anticipation of getting a response to posts on social media and found there was a 400% spike in Dopamine. Remember Dopamine is addictive.

The dangers grow when we start believing the fake/airbrushed images of others' lives and comparing ours to theirs. People can experience feelings of isolation, withdrawal being inadequate and so on.

Remember: once something is posted on the internet – it's never really deleted!

Dangers in the world of work. The fake world of social media can intrude as follows:

- In meetings – mobiles kept on the table, says 'neither you nor this meeting is really important to me'. A much more potent message is sent by keeping your mobile on silent and out of sight,

- Waiting to go into a meeting or for someone to join, we check our phones rather than talk to each other. Because we don't talk to each other and build relationships we don't help each other as much as we could.

- It is believed ideas come from freeing the brain to wander, which it can't do if we're always on social media

- Life is not instant. You have to work at building a fulfilling career and relationships. You have to see the joy in everyday life. Social media often prevents this.

- The increase of mental health issues amongst those addicted to social media is rising substantially.

DIGITAL DEMENTIA

Again, strong evidence proves we give up working our brains and taking the easy route of using our mobiles. How often do you use your mobile's calculator to work out something like what portion of a bill you pay when out with friends instead of doing it in your head?

The brain is like any other 'body part'. If you don't use it, it stops working. In the brains case, it's permanent. Hence the scary, but accurate term of 'digital dementia'.

Warning signs you may need to make changes:

• Do you text as you walk?
• Do you check your phone each morning before literally doing anything else?
• Do you have to check how many 'likes'/'dislikes' you've received just after posting?
• Are your friends real or just on-line?
• Can you ever leave your mobile at home?
• Do you feel more comfortable starting a conversation with a human face-to- face or via social media chat?
• Do you take your mobile with you everywhere, including into every room at home?
• Do you keep your mobile on your desk whilst working?
• Do you regularly have 'tech free' time?

There is nothing wrong with using Social Media. It's often really helpful. Using it to excess can be harmful. Be mindful of how you use it.

December 2019 brought muted whispers of a virus spreading from Wuhan in China. A young doctor working there had raised concerns about the number of deaths – unusually high – with the same viral symptoms. He died of this new virus.

January/February 2020, the virus reared its head in the UK. There wasn't a huge amount of information. It was looked on as a new form of flu. Suddenly the rates of death amongst the older/vulnerable population started to rise and the Government had to take notice. 23 March 2020 saw a national lockdown. It was also day two of the orientation week of Growing Talent's 26th programme held in London. It was thought at the time this would be a short lockdown to protect the NHS before the virus was defeated. Little did we know.

January 2021 the virus is still rampaging and the UK is effectively in another national lockdown after trying differ tier systems, keeping universities and schools open then shutting them, no large gatherings etc. Nothing seemed to work. Family events have been stopped from birthday parties, weddings, summer BBQs to funerals. The Aviation and Hospitality sectors have been ravished. Millions have been furloughed. Many have lost their jobs – many have lost a lot more. Temporary state benefit increases have been brought in to help low income families along with food hampers/vouchers for children who were entitled to free school meals. Each has caused massive issues with some falling through the gaps of state support. Mental health issues have increased across the board.

December 2020 brought a beacon of light with the introduction of authorised vaccines. The first to be released was a collaboration between Pfizer and BioNTech. This vaccine has to be stored at very low temperatures not in a standard fridge like the majority of vaccines are. The JCVI (Joint Committee on Vaccine Immunisation) set out steps for demographics of the UK to be immunised in order to bring down the death rates effectively. The most vulnerable group were the over 80s. Many people in this group have mobility issues making travel to immunisation centres difficult. GPs and community nursing staff have a short window to administer the vaccine once it's out of refrigeration. Shortly after this vaccine release, a second easier to store one followed produced by Astrazenneca and Oxford University. Now the rollout of JVCI's set groups could ramp up. The Government set a figure of 15million people to receive a first vaccine by 15 February 2021 – which was achieved.

The vaccines have shown cross country collaboration is possible to defeat the global pandemic which fills me with hope for the future defeat of cancers, dementia, environmental and other human issues through this type of collaboration if humankind learn the lessons from this pandemic and continue to work together.

During the virtual Open Mic Drop-in sessions, I've been running for a client's frontline teams, it's become clear how much misinformation is causing fear and sleepless nights from social media, community groups even from family and friends to those considering having the vaccine. Trouble is negativity spreads and negative thoughts amplify – especially at night – especially where people live alone.

It's perfectly natural to question whether to have the vaccine or not. There is a lot of fake information circulating on Social Media, within our communities and by own family/friends. Mainstream media news is full of doom. All of this can make it hard to think clearly and logically. Whirling thoughts can keep us awake at night, physically and emotionally draining us.

Traditionally, new medicines and vaccines have taken years to reach market. MHRA -the authorisation body in the UK for this responsibility - executed the process for these vaccines in a matter of months. MHRA (Medicines and Healthcare products Regulatory Agency) explained on national TV and media outlets how they undertook multiple processes simultaneously to speed up the process without skipping any regulatory steps because it was a global pandemic. Makes me wonder why they can't use this new process for other medicines. Will they going forward?

So, what can we do ourselves?

1.   Ensure you listen only to qualified sources.
2.   Look at the national and global evidence.
3.   Discuss any fears with your GP.
4.   Make your decision based on what is right for you, not what those around you say.

Points to consider:

- Fear sells. In 1998 Dr Andrew Wakefield wrote a paper stating his research showed a connection between the then new MMR vaccine and the development of Autism. This research was later discredited. Dr Wakefield was struck off. Today, 23 years later, some parents still fear this research and choose not to have their child vaccinated. The consequences for some have been devastating.

- What is the vaccine really made of? Go to www.gov.uk and use the search box to find the ingredient list for each vaccine being used in the UK for Covid19.

- Any adverse effects to the vaccines are reported by the public and can be viewed by everyone under MHRA's Yellow Card site: https://yellowcard.mhra.gov.uk click on the Covid19 tab, scroll down you will see a link to a published report of side effects. Those reported are the usual symptoms people get following all vaccines.

- If the Covid vaccines are so harmful, why is the world using them and the World Health Organisation (WHO) endorsing them to be used in the way the UK is? BMJ (British Medical Journal) has lots of reference information https://www.bmj.com/content/372/bmj.n338 WHO website gives a global view www.who.int

One key area of concern is the amount of people who have 'enjoyed' being furloughed or on increased benefits who now fear going back to working outside the home again. Understandable but essential for mental wellbeing and social mobility.

Looking at magazines fashion spreads which used to be clothes for the office, going out or weekend casuals, are now filled with casual homeworking – tracksuits, pjs etc. The thinking appears to be you only need to look 'presentable' from the neck up for virtual meetings.

The majority of people are becoming physically and mentally poorer. Eating too much and drinking alcohol much more than they used to whilst moving much less. Personal hygiene routines are reduced due to 'what's the point?' impacting negatively.

So how do we get out of the quicksand of facing our fears to be ready to go back to the workplace?

One key area I feel is to start getting work routines in place NOW before having to go back to the workplace. As we learned earlier, we have to create a routine – doing something at the same time each day for three weeks before it becomes an automatic habit. We also know we are never going to feel like doing it, so we have to force ourselves to by utilising tools learned earlier including the 5,4,3,2,1 trick.

Start with getting up at the time we used to when we worked outside the home and showering to energise us. Taking care of our skin and hair, applying any make-up every day the same as when we 'went' to work outside the home. Putting on clean clothes – maybe not the suits you used to wear but steer away from tracksuits/onesies/pjs.

Go to work at a desk/table in your room/home enables you to step away for breaks more easily than using your laptop in your living room whilst having the tv on in the background creating massive distraction and blurs the lines of your home and work environments. Chiropractors say working at home means you are more likely not to be working at an appropriate desk with an adjustable chair so get up and move around every 15-20 minutes. Take a lunchbreak each day away from the screens.

As the restrictions start to lift, start leaving home and walking to your local station as though you were getting the train to work. Do this each day will get you exercise, free your mind and get you more confident to return to working outside your home again. After a week or so, start travelling to your place of work. Do this a few times when it's quieter to get your confidence up on using public transport again.

If anxiety is rising, utilise some of the tools illustrated earlier in the selfcare toolbox such as listening to music on your mobile, power breathing or consider meeting up with a friend/work colleague on route to travel in together. As restrictions lift further and your employer is ready for you to return, you will be confident and ready. Equally, if you are seeking a new job, your confidence will be that much higher preparing for it in advance. If wearing a mask and gloves gives you more confidence and security use them as long as you want to whether restrictions are in place or not.

The key is small steps. Don't overthink the return to work. Setting the small targets above will empower you to achieve the overall goal of getting back. Planning something fun like a future holiday in the sun gives you a goal to save for and a purpose to work. Just make sure it's fully refundable. Look at everything you've conquered in your life. This is just another moment you **WILL** overcome.

We can consider this a 'once in a lifetime' event but humankind's history shows we don't always learn from events leading to them being repeated. Hopefully the intense devastation caused by the Covid19 pandemic will enable us to learn core lessons. One thing is clear, we have no control on how governments globally handle a pandemic or any crisis but we can control how we look at it and reduce the impact on us personally. Never has the mantra 'it's not what happens to us that impacts us but how we think about those things' been more apt.

My hope for myself, family, friends – everyone, regardless of their background from this experience is we nurture ourselves with positivity and acceptance going forward and more kindness to others.

AD HOC THOUGHTS

Grab every opportunity! You will work out a way of doing it. Don't turn down any opportunity just because 'you don't know how' – you can learn.

Someone presented me with an opportunity to start my own business. What did I know about starting a business? – nothing! Even more interesting was I had to have it set-up in seven days!

So, I made a plan. Searched out a local Accountant. Decided on a bank I wanted to hold my business account. Decided on a name for the business. The Accountant registered the business at Companies House, did all the paperwork, registered me for VAT with HMRC and gave me a lot of information to read.

My limited company was set-up and registered with all relevant parties within seven days. Over seven years later, I'm thankful to say it's still going.

Remember people will not always say what they mean! Be prepared to have a discussion to ensure you understand what they were trying to say.

News and TV reports will always go with unbalanced headlines which sell their stories. The audience will generally form an opinion without considering what the whole picture might be.

Always stop and think what is the other side of the argument. It helps form a balanced opinion.

Kindness rules! It's been proven scientifically to be good for our health and immune system. Maya Angelou once said *'people will forget what you said, but they will never forget how you made them feel'*. How do you want people to remember you?

Head on – sometimes you have to make a stand as a matter of integrity and principle. Focus on that to get you through.

Even if the situation drags on for years and people tell you to give up and walk away, keep going. If we give up on our principles and integrity, what have we got?

Find your passion! I fell into commercial recruitment which led to inclusive employment which led to the Real Apprentice – which won multiple awards and brought speaking opportunities at the House of Commons on mental health and employment – which led to Growing Talent which was put on hold with Coronavirus which led to reflection of where I want to be and a plan to get there.

Being part of someone's journey to empowerment and helping them find the strength to change their life has been my passion and honour but it was never something I consciously set out to do.

Remember - every opportunity leads other opportunities with exciting challenges and learning inbetween.

It's not about the money! I've been in financial straits and financially comfortable at different times in my life. What I've learnt is the people who matter are those that are only interested in the most priceless gift you can give to them - your time. Judge yourself by your heart, empathy and courage not material things.

Entrepreneurial spirit – if you've decided to set your own business up, remember tax is now digital with the use of bespoke software like QuickBooks and Xero is now mandatory.

These involve live bank feeds from your business bank account. Before choosing which software to use, check with your bank which they support. If you don't and use one, they don't support, it can invalidate their T&Cs

A last thought I would like to leave you with – *always look forward, never back – it's time for you to rise-up and move forward.*

HELPFUL ORGANISATIONS FOR LIFE ISSUES

Crisis Situations
Give Us A Shout – 24/7 crisis text line for any issue. Text the word Shout to 85258. Completely free. For all ages.
Stay Alive App – free suicide prevention app developed by Grassroots Suicide Prevention. For use by those thinking of suicide and those supporting someone who is suicidal.
Samaritans – 24/7 freephone service 116123. E-mail: jo@samaritans.org
CALM (Campaign Against Living Miserably) www.thecalmzone.net support via webchat or phone line – 0800 585858 for men in distress or crisis. Open 5pm to midnight.

Finding a therapist
British Psychological Society www.bps.org.uk
British Association for Counselling & Psychotherapy Register www.itsgoodtotalk.org.uk
IAPT (Improving Access to Psychological Therapies) search IAPT in Google for your local one. In London it's SLAM 0203 228 2194

Abuse (domestic violence, child, sexual abuse, financial abuse)
NAPAC www.napc.org.uk National Association for People Abused in Childhood. Support on line and free resources.
NSPCC www.nspcc.org.uk – aims to end child abuse and cruelty also runs Childline 0800 1111. Adults concerned a child may be at risk of abuse can call 0800 800 5000
Rape Crisis – www.rapecrisis.org.uk
Refuge – www.refuge.org.uk 0808 2000 247 24/7 freephone domestic violence helpline. Also links to FGM, honour based violence, forced marriage and human trafficking.
True Vision – any kind of hate crime www.report-it.org.uk
Bright Sky app – download from www.hestia.org for anyone in an abusive relationship whose phone may be monitored. This app looks like a weather app to anyone else.
Men only experiencing abuse from family, partners, ex-partners – anyone www.mensadviceline.org.uk 0808 8010327
999 – police emergency. If dangerous to talk, press 55. Police track through the open line.

Addiction
Adfam – support for families affected by substance abuse. www.adfam.org.uk
AA – www.alcoholics-anonymous.org.uk
Drinkline 0300 123 1110 freephone 9am-8pm Monday-Friday. 11am-4pm Weekends.
Talk to Frank – www.talktofrank.com information and support on drugs for teenagers and adolescents

Anxiety
www.anxietyuk.org.uk – talking therapies and self-help groups
www.ocdaction.org.uk - OCD Action online support and advocacy services
www.topuk.org – Triumph Over Phobia
www.bigwhitewall.com – also available as an app. Supports those not coping well with anxiety

Bereavement

www.bereavementadvice.org – Bereavement Advice Centre practical advice and support

www.childereavementuk.org – Supports families affected by the death of a child

www.uksobs.org – supports those bereaved by suicide

BiPolar

www.bipolaruk.org

Carers

www.carers.org – Carers Trust - support for all carers including those under 18

www.carersuk.org – Carers UK – practical, financial and emotional help for all carers

Depression

www.depressionuk.org – national self-help for those experiencing depression.

Eating disorders

www.b-eat.co.uk – also have dedicated helplines and peer to peer support.

General

www.mind.org.uk range of services including signposting to local organisations

www.rethink.org – advice and information services

www.youngminds.org – for young people and their parents/carers

LGBT

www.switchboard.lgbt – confidential support and referrals services including on-line chat.

Personality disorders

www.emergenceplus.org.uk – service user led supports users, carers, family, friends and professionals.

Relationahips

www.family-action.org.uk – emotional and financial support to families experiencing hardship

www.relate.org.uk – couple and family support.

Self-Harm

www.harmless.org.uk – user led provides a range of services includes alternative coping strategies. www.selfharm.co.uk a safe space to talk and ask questions

Sleep

www.nhs.uk – links to information including Every Mind Matters, sleep better techniques and free apps

Worried about young people

www.place2be.org.uk – help for primary and secondary ages

www.childline.org.uk – free and confidential counselling for children 24/7 helpline 0800 1111

www.youngminds.org.uk – support for young people. Parent's helpline is available 9.30am-4pm Monday-Friday – 0808 802 5544.

Worried about Co-Vid 19
www.nhs.uk/oneyou/every-mind-matters/coronavirus-covid-19-anxiety-tips - 10 top tips to manage fears during lockdown. Will also help with anxiety in general – not just Coronavirus/Co-Vid19 related.

Note: all of the above organisations were accurate at the time of publishing.

SIGNPOSTING FOR SETTING-UP A BUSINESS

Check out the Government's free website www.gov.uk/browse/business/setting-up
This gives a lot of information and signposting including:

- Writing a business plan
- Help and support available for your business
- Start-up loans that may be available for your business
- Implications of tax and registration options for your business:
    Sole trader
    Limited Company
    Business Partnership
    Social Enterprise

This is a great, free resource to flesh out your ideas and highlight areas you may not have considered.

Accountant

It's important to use a qualified accountant registered with a regulatory body. You can check their registers for qualified accountants in your area. Your relationship with your accountant is important. Take the time to visit a few to ensure your feel comfortable. Most accountants will give a free short meeting for this purpose. Afterall, they want to make sure they want to work with you too!

ICAEW – Institute of Chartered Accounts in England and Wales
General.enquiries@icaew.com
020 7920 8100

IFA (Independent Financial Advisor)

In addition to an accountant, you may want investment advice for pensions, savings etc. It's important to make sure anyone you select is qualified and regulated.

You can check this at www.register.fca.org.uk to search their name and location against the register.

If you are referred to an IFA by a friend/family member, take the time to meet them first to see they are someone you can work with as well as checking they are listed on the FCA register and therefore qualified and regulated. Remember you are entrusting your financial decisions to them so the relationship has to be right.

If you have no recommendations, you can start your search on www.unbiased.co.uk, www.moneysavingsexpert.com www.moneysupermarket.com – again meet anyone and check they are on the register before signing up with them.

Private Pension Advisor

Looking to the future, ultimately having your own pension pot and not just relying on the state pension is a good idea. It's vital to secure the right professional advice.

The Government's free money advise service has a directory of regulated advisors for pensions/retirement financial planning.

www.directry.moneyadviceservice.org.uk

WORKPLACE SCENARIOS - ANSWERS

Compare your thoughts with those below. Did you agree?

Case study 1

You like your own company. Your employer is having a BBQ in the grounds of their warehouse where you work as a porter. Your role entails all duties in the warehouse. You joined at the same time as four others who work in different departments upstairs. As the five of you are new to the company, your employer gives you all an early finish to go home and change before the BBQ later. You choose not to return but don't tell anyone. Afterall, they won't miss you.

On returning to work the following day, you are asked to clean-up the BBQ and store it at the back of the warehouse. You refuse as you didn't attend the BBQ you don't see why you should clean it.

Was that the right action? No. Your job entails all areas of the warehouse. Therefore, you have to clean the BBQ and store it away whether you went to the event or not.

Was there something else you could have done? If you'd been honest and said you weren't attending the BBQ, they would not have spent time trying to track you down to make sure you were safe under their duty of care. In addition, they may view you as not completely honest as you kept quiet to keep the early finish. This thoughtless action could have damaged your prospects.

Case study 2

With a love of cooking, you secure your dream job in a corporate kitchen where your employer is going to send you for formal training at their cost. There's a huge amount of potential for your career. One of your new ideas for as dessert were incorporated to last week's menu giving great feedback.

The manager wants you to speak at his corporate client's meeting on how your journey is going. This is out of your comfort zone. You don't like public speaking.

What do you say? Always say 'yes' to every opportunity.

Why? We have no idea where opportunities can lead. We learn from every opportunity we accept and nothing from those we refuse. Facing our fear is better than avoiding it. The manager only wants me to speak about my journey. I'll be speaking about a something I know about!

Case study 3

After three years spent unemployed, you are selected for a training opportunity which has a permanent job attached to it. You are the eldest living at home. Your mum has five other children including a two year old. To your knowledge, she has never worked bringing you all up as a single parent has left her with little support, a diagnosis of depression and medication. She relies on you and wants you to stay at home to help her.

What goes through your mind? Conflicted. This is the best opportunity for me but my mum relies on me so much.

What can you do? Consider getting some help for mum. Reach out to wider family – aunts/uncles, her GP, local community groups. Your mum needs help to deal with her depression and move on without negatively impacting your life. Seeking help and encouraging her to accept it is the best solution to you both getting independence.

Case study 4

It's the third week in your new job – which you love. However, you sense a chill in the air whenever Sarah, your Supervisor, is nearby. During the first week, there was a team chat on politics. You and Sarah completely disagreed. Things got a little heated. There's been a 'chill' since this.

What can you do? Seems to be two choices here. Ignore it and hope it dies away or speak to Sarah about what happened, how you both feel and a way to resolve the bad atmosphere.

When we disagree with someone, it's critical to ensure we are clear it's their view we disagree with not their whole person. A subtle, but key difference.

What are the consequences of doing nothing? The atmosphere will spread and be noticed. By the wider team if it hasn't already. You may get to the point of leaving the job you love because of it.

Case study 5

You work in a busy office in the heart of the City. It's a new role – just your first week! Your manager gives you several tasks to complete before lunch. They will be in meetings but you have their mobile number.

The Supervisor asks you to come and help the distribution team unload a delivery which is blocking the road outside. The team there is understaff due to sickness and traffic is backing up.

The manager's mobile is on answerphone. If you have the distribution team out, you won't complete your tasks.

What do you do? Leave a message on your manager's mobile then support the Supervisor and team. Completing the Manager's set tasks on your return.

Why? The Supervisor will take responsibility of what's is a priority. You will show the Manager and Supervisor you are a team player and adaptable to situations as they arise. The distribution team will remember you helped them and return the favour in the future when you need it.

Case study 6

It's your third day in your new job. Everything has gone wrong. The alarm didn't go off. Rushing around you didn't eat breakfast and picked up yesterday's top. Despite chasing the bus, you missed it. Now you are going to be late. Sweating, uncomfortable and embarrassed you finally arrive just 15 minutes late.

The manager is not impressed.

What could you have done to avoid this situation? Always call ahead if you think you may be late but make sure you get the name of the person you speak to and time you made the call. Prepare and set out your clothes and breakfast things the night before. Set two alarms and aim at earlier transport options to get you into work in good time even if there are traffic delays – you can always settle and have a tea/coffee before starting work if you arrive a little early.

Case study 7

It's the day of your appraisal. Your manager hasn't been around much but you are confident it will go well. The manager raises two performance issues with you. The first was arriving late on site. The second was returning late from lunch. This is a shock to you. Afterall you had called ahead and spoke to the team when you knew you would be late due to traffic and Sue in the team saw you go to help a senior manager who had dropped some files making you late returning from lunch. Surely these messages had been passed on? You start to get upset.

What do you say? Number one rule – NEVER have any conversation at work or at home when you are upset. You won't think clearly. In this instance say what a shock it is to hear this and request a delay in the appraisal allowing you to gather your thoughts. The manager will not make you have a conversation once you've explained this and made the request.

What could you consider doing going forward to avoid this again? Never assume people will pass messages on. When calling into the office, get the name of the team member taking your call and note the time you made the call. When you arrive on site, make sure you speak with the manager to apologise and explain you spoke with 'so and so' at 7.30am. The manager will be aware you did everything possible and won't penalise you on your next appraisal. The same applies to being late returning from lunch. Explain to the manager what happened either in person or via email. Helping others is admirable especially senior management of the company as it raises the reputation of your department.

REFERENCES

Dr Amy Cuddy – American Social Psychologist, Author, TEDTalk Speaker Professor and Researcher at Harvard Business School.

Simon Sinek – Author and inspirational speaker, TEDTalk speaker https://simonsinek.com

David Mead – Co Author of Find Your Why with Simon Sinek above. David is an international thought leader.

Mel Robbins – American tv host, author, motivational speaker https://melrobbins.com

Richard Alderson set up Careershifters to help those changing careers/industries www.careershifters.org

Page 49 – the 7%-38%-55% rule devised by Professor Albert Mehrabian

Table on page 50 illustrates agreed results of various research papers over decades including a feature by Raphael Ahmed for the British Council 18.5.15 and Extension University of Missouri publication by Dick Lee and Delmar Hateshol.

With Grateful Thanks To: Kat Davis & Shennell Arko Dadzie for their views on this book. May your light always shine bright.

Printed in Great Britain
by Amazon